Small Business Management in Developing Countries

Small Business Management in Developing Countries

Management problems with reference to policy environment, institutional framework and UNIDO technical assistance

Luke Ike

Copyright © 2018 by Luke Ike.

ISBN: Softcover   978-1-5434-9095-4
             eBook   978-1-5434-9094-7

All rights reserved. No part of this book may be reproduced or transmitted in any form or by any means, electronic or mechanical, including photocopying, recording, or by any information storage and retrieval system, without permission in writing from the copyright owner.

Any people depicted in stock imagery provided by Getty Images are models, and such images are being used for illustrative purposes only.
Certain stock imagery © Getty Images.

Print information available on the last page.

Rev. date: 06/12/2018

To order additional copies of this book, contact:
Xlibris
800-056-3182
www.Xlibrispublishing.co.uk
Orders@Xlibrispublishing.co.uk
778387

CONTENTS

Introduction To The Book xi

PART 1
THE NATURE OF SMALL BUSINESS IN DEVELOPING COUNTRIES (DCs)

Introduction 3

Chapter 1: Introduction To Small Business In Developing
             Countries (Dcs) 5
   1.1 Definitions 6
   1.2 Characteristics of Small Business 11
   1.3 Characteristics of Small Business in Developing
       Countries 13
   Further reading 17

Chapter 2: Relative Significance And Potential Roles Of
             Small Business In Developing Countries (Dcs) 18
   2.1 Introduction 19
   2.2 Employment 20
   2.3 Income Distribution 23
   2.4 Regional Distribution of Industries and Development 24
   2.5 Linkages 25
   2.6 Maintaining Competition 28
   2.7 Capital Building 29
   2.8 Production for a Particular Local Market 30
   2.9 Innovation 31
   2.10 Savings 32
   2.11 Improving the Entrepreneurial Role of Women 33
   2.12 Mobilising Indigenous Entrepreneurship 36
   Further reading 37

PART 2
THE ENVIRONMENT OF SMALL BUSINESS IN DEVELOPING COUNTRIES (DCs)

Introduction 41

Chapter 3: The Policy Environment For Small Business In
Developing Countries (Dcs) 43

    3.1 Introduction 44
    3.2 Policy Objectives 45
    3.3 Policy Measures 49
    Further reading 54

Chapter 4: The Institutional Framework For Small Business
In Developing Countries (Dcs) 55

    4.1 Introduction 56
    4.2 Technical and Industrial Advisory/ Extension
        Institutions 57
    4.3 Industrial Research Institutions 60
    4.4 Finance and Credit Service Institutions 61
    4.5 Common Facility Centers 64
    4.6 Small Business Marketing Institutions 66
    4.7 Small Business Interest Serving Associations 68
    4.8 Institutions And Programmes For Small Business In
        Nigeria 70
    Further reading 88

PART 3
MANAGEMENT PROBLEMS OF SMALL BUSINESS IN DEVELOPING COUNTRIES (DCs)

Introduction 91

Chapter 5: The Nature Of Management 93

    5.1 Introduction 94
    5.2 Management Fundamentals 95

5.3 The Small Business Performance in Developing
    Countries (DCs) 98
Further reading 99

Chapter 6: Sources Of Management Problems Of Small
           Business In Developing Countries (Dcs) 100

6.1 Introduction..101
6.2 External Environment 102
6.2.1 Policy Weaknesses...102
6.2.2 Institutional Weaknesses...109
6.2.3 Infrastructure 115
6.3 Internal Environment...118
6.3.1 Finance 118
6.3.2 Production 123
6.3.3 Personnel..125
6.3.4 Marketing 127
6.3.5 The Small Business Owner/Manager 131
Further reading 133

PART 4
TECHNICAL ASSISTANCE AND SMALL BUSINESS IN DEVELOPING COUNTRIES (DCs)

Introduction..137

Chapter 7: Technical Assistance And Small Business In Dcs..........139

7.1 Introduction..140
7.2 Technical Assistance - Definitions...............................141
7.3 Technical Assistance and Aid 144
7.4 Forms of Technical Assistance....................................145
Further reading 147

Chapter 8: The Unido/Undp Technical Assistance For Small
           Busines In Dcs 148

8.1 The UNIDO/UNDP Technical Assistance....................149
8.2 UNIDO Response to Small Business Management
    Problems in Developing Countries (DCs) 157

8.3 Errors and Problems Associated with Technical
      Assistance Projects in Developing Countries...................162
Further reading 166

PART 5
IMPROVING SMALL BUSINESS MANAGEMENT AND PERFORMANCE IN DEVELOPING COUNTRIES (DCs)

Introduction..169

Chapter 9: Achieving Small Business Management And
                Performance In Dcs.....................................171

    9.1 Introduction...172
    9.2 External Environment 173
    9.2.1 Policy Environment..173
    9.2.2 Institutional Framework...183
    9.2.3 UNIDO Technical Assistance..................................187
    9.3 Internal Environment...190
    9.3.1 Finance 190
    9.3.2 Marketing 194
    9.3.3 Personnel...198
    9.3.4 The Small Business Owner/Manager 201
    9.3.5 Production 204
    Further reading 209

References 211

AKNOWLEDGEMENTS

This book is dedicated to the memory of my beloved father Hyacinth, my beloved mother Eunice and my beloved sister Philomena.

Luke Ike

INTRODUCTION TO THE BOOK

This book aims at making a contribution to the promotion of small business in developing countries.

The current interest in small business by many developing countries (DCs), as a special industrialisation strategy, is the main motive for this book.

Several efforts in terms of various country-internal policy incentives/measures and institutions have so far been committed to the promotion of small business in many developing countries (DCs).

These efforts have been complemented by external technical assistance provided particularly by United Nations Industrial Development Organisation (UNIDO).

While all these efforts are commendable, literature reviews indicate that small businesses are faced with management problems of various kinds considering the low level of their industrial performance.

These management problems encountered by small businesses in DCs contribute directly or indirectly to the sofar poor performance of this business sector to the national economic development of many DCs.

In the course of their development in DCs, it becomes very necessary to have current and adequate knowledge of the type of management problems small businesses are facing in DCs so that possibly, immediate and appropriate correction and improvements can be made.

This book will be making valuable contributions to this effect. It will do so by helping to identify the current management problems facing small businesses in various DCs -with regards to policies/measures and institutions provided with special reference to the institutional aspect of technical assistance provided by UNIDO.

The result of this work is aimed at helping to provide a good information base for individuals who are already in the small business sector and those interested in it.

PART 1

THE NATURE OF SMALL BUSINESS IN DEVELOPING COUNTRIES (DCS)

INTRODUCTION

For a proper understanding and discussion of the management problems of small business in developing countries (DCs) and subsequent appropriate recommendations, it is necessary to first of all know actually what constitutes small business in general and those operating in the DCs in particular.

This introductory chapter will deal with the general and special areas of Small businesses in developing countries. First, general characteristics of small businesses will be briefly discussed, followed by a full insight into the special characteristics of small businesses found in DCs. The role of small business will also be introduced and discussed fully.

CHAPTER 1

INTRODUCTION TO SMALL BUSINESS IN DEVELOPING COUNTRIES (DCS)

Aim

To introduce the nature of small business in developing countries.

Objectives

After studying this chapter you should be able to:

- Understand the meaning of small business.
- Understand characteristics of small business.
- Describe characteristics of small business in developing countries.

1.1 Definitions

It is difficult to come by a concise and universally accepted definition of small business. What is regarded small in one country may be seen as big in another. The term "small" is therefore very relative and definition to this respect differs from one country to another and even with institutions in a given country. Each country or institutions tends to drive its definition based on the role small businesses are expected to play in the economy and the programme of assistance being designed for them.

Various criteria have been used in defining small business in various countries and within different institutions that are concerned with small business establishment and development. Some of the criteria used in the definition include:

- ✓ Employment.
- ✓ Capital investment.
- ✓ Annual turnover.
- ✓ Ownership and management functions.
- ✓ Combination of criteria.
- ✓ Unofficial criteria or differing criteria.
- ✓ Combination of small and medium scale (SMEs).

Depending on the country or institution in question, these criteria could be qualitative or quantitively differeciated or dimensionally applied.

The criterion (criteria) used in given period of time is usually chosen according to the purpose of classification or identification - statistical, policy, assistance, research, rational, legal prescription, special assistance, etc.

Employment

In many developing countries, the use of employment has been very popular.

In Indonesia for example, the Indonesian Bureau of Statistics has been classifying small businesses as those establishment employing 5 - 9 workers (since the census of 1974 - 1975).

In Columbia, the small business is defined as one employing between10-49 workers.

In Peru, the small business is defined as one employing less than 50 workers.

In Kenya, the small business is officially defined as one employing 3 - 50 workers.

Capital investment

Capital investment has also been used by many countries and governments in developing countries to identify the small business for a particular purpose or agenda.

In India, the official definition of small business by the Indian Government and Small Industries Development Organisation (SIDO) has always been based on the initial investment capital in plant and machinery (in many cases not exceeding Rs 2 Million). Small businesses defined in this manner are heavily concentrated in and around the urban areas as the sector excludes village industry.

In Zambia, small businesses are defined as industries having capital assets of less than 250,000 kwacha.

In Nigeria, the National Economic Reconstruction Fund (NERFUND) defines small business as those with total assets value (excluding land) of not more than ten million naira.

Turnover

In Nigeria for example, the Central Bank of Nigeria (CBN) in relation to the CBN credit guidance, defines as small any business whose annual turnover ranges from between one naira to fifty thousand naira.

Combination of criteria

While the use of employment is frequent, there are countries and institutions in developing countries applying a combination of criteria.

For example, in Senegal, small businesses are defined as those with a workforce of 5 - 50 and an investment level of between 5 - 25 million CFA.

In the Philippines, small businesses are defined officially in term of functions, total assets and level of employment. Small businesses in this area are defined as those enterprises in which the owner/manager is not actively engaged in production but performs the varied range of tasks involved in guidance and leadership without the help of specialist staff, and with total assets mainly, in the range of P50, 000 to P5 million.

In Senegal, small businesses are defined as those with a workforce of 5-50 and an investment level of between 5-25 million CFA.

In Tanzania, small businesses have been defined using different criteria for different purpose:

- ✓ In terms of units whose control is within the people (individually or collectively).
- ✓ In terms of location and capital required - located in the villages, with fixed assets not exceeding 1 million Tanzanian shillings.
- ✓ In terms of employment, (1) a non factory industry (up to 10 workers), (2) factory type small scale industry (10-50 workers).

In Nigeria, the Federal Ministry of Industry's small scale division defines a small business as one whose total capital outlay is below sixty thousand naira and whose total employees are not more than fifty.

Combination of small and medium businesses (SMEs)

Apart from differences in the use of criteria, small and medium scale industries are sometimes defined together in many developing countries.

In Singapore for example, small and medium enterprise (SMEs) are defined together by the Small and Medium Scale Enterprises Division in the Economic Development Board (EDB) as those being locally registered, with at least 30% local equity, and less than US$ 8 million in fixed assets, including machinery and equipment.

In Nigeria small and medium enterprises as defined by the Central Bank of Nigeria (CBN) are economically independent companies with 11 to 300 employees and an annual turnover of between 5 to 500 million naira.

It is important to mention here that the absence of concise uniform definition of the concept of small business is not peculiar to the developing countries alone. There are developed countries

And international institutions that apply varied criteria to achieve their purpose for the small business. In U.S. for example, most firms are considered small if they have not more than 500 employees. Also in Germany and France, small and medium scale industries also fall under the group of industries employing not more than 500 workers.

In UK criteria adopted by the Bolton report include a combination of:

- ✓ Size - turnover, net capital or balance sheet, number of employees
- ✓ Economic and control - market share, independence, personal management (these are not popular with developing countries).

International organisations like the World Bank, ILO, UNIDO and UNDP have all used employees to define small businesses at various times to suit various purposes. For example, research carried out in 1988 by UNIDO/UNDP in conjunction with the ILO and the government of the Netherland, for the purpose of research, identification and possible technical assistance, defined small businesses as those employing 5-25 workers or employees.

Conclusion

The free use of various criteria, singly or in combination, by different countries and institutions, as observed above, underlines the difficulty in the application of a universally accepted definition. In addition, there are also areas where small and medium scale industries are defined together leaving no clear distinction (as in Singapore).

Another side-effect is the problem in getting reliable data on small business in developing countries, which makes research and other related activities burdensome.

All these create the problem of arriving at a clear definition, as well as application or implementation of special activities for small businesses in developing countries. *The importance of clear definition of small business therefore cannot be overemphasized.*

The use of different criteria by many developing countries is also not without limitations. A critical aspect of using only employment as a criterion in defining a small business is that this could be highly illusory. Due to the use of computers, robots or other production machinery, most large scale projects can still be handled by a reasonable number of personnel. It is also important to note that the use of capital costs or turnover as the main criteria may ignore the influence of inflation on capital investments, or the fact that different projects have diverse capital/output rations.

Recognizing these problems, it is important to take the benefit of revision of any accepted definition from time to time, to make identifiable small businesses that share some familiar problems.

For the purpose of this book, small businesses are defined as those having *less than 50 employees* operating in urban or rural areas, and involved in production of goods and services.

1.2 Characteristics of Small Business

Small businesses are not just scale- down versions of large ones. They have some special characteristics that set them apart and make the process of management different from that of large firms. These characteristics also make most small firms inherently riskier than large firms:

These characteristics include:

- Owned and managed by one person.
- Tends to be labour intensive.
- Unlikely to be able to exert much influence in the market.
- Likely to operate in a single market.
- Likely to be over reliance on a small number of customers.
- Not public limited companies (plc).
- Not homogenous.

Generally, small businesses are typically financed by an individual, his friends or relatives. This is due to many problems these businesses encounter in obtaining credit from established financial institutions and association especially, the commercial banks. Impelled by their personal concern for the venture, they usually put together funds wherever they can find them to start or run their small business.

Their limited access to finance is reflected in the low level of fixed investment assets and therefore, they tend to be more labor intensive with a low capital/labor ratio.

They are also known to have close contacts with their workers, the market and local resources due to the fact that their level of employment is small.

In most cases small businesses operate in small and mostly local market, usually producing to the wishes of their customers.

Although most small businesses lack bargaining power relative to larger industries, their small size, their low operating fixed cost, and the close personal contacts with workers and the market are, when used properly, a source of strength in many ways. They offer some advantages, prominent of which are flexibility and adaptability to the market place. Many small businesses remain small because they have functions to perform that are impossible or impractical for large industries.

Frequently, small businesses operate for limited, mostly local market.

In some cases, some small businesses are small by choice, seeking to remain strong personal contact; others because they are specialist in limited field, and some business by nature can never become large.

Usually, the organizational structure of a small business is simple, informal and portrays a "one man band" – type, mostly owner managed. There normally many types of small businesses making them a homogenous group seeking finance privately and therefore, privately owned, and have less access to public sources of finance available to larger firms- such as the Stock Exchange Markets.

It is sometimes asked, "Will not the large scale industries drive out the small ones?", and "Can the small business really stand the large scale industries in this period of a fast and tough, changing and dynamically competitive industrial world?"

The answer is that many small businesses can and do compete quite successfully. This relates to their peculiar characteristics which gives them the advantages of flexibility, adaptability innovation, etc.

Small, they say is "beautiful". Every large scale business was once small. The strategy of smallness has usually formed the base for industrialisation in the earlier attempts at economic development of any nation. Large scale industries could be said to be in many ways a characteristic feature of modern industrial economy although they are not the whole of it. However, a country will have the most productive industrial structures when it has an interwoven combination of large and small scale industries in which the place of each is determined on basis of economic efficiency.

1.3 Characteristics of Small Business in Developing Countries

Reviewing the characteristics of small business operating in developing countries (DCs) in particular, will help us pictures some of their advantages as well as weaknesses. This relates in most cases to their general characteristics, which are essential for recognizing small businesses in developing countries, reflecting in many ways, the roles the small business can play in the economy of any country, depending on the level of the development of the business environment in which they operate.

Specifically, the types of small businesses found in developed countries have some differences to those found in developing countries (DCs). This is because this business sector operates in an environment which is in many ways different from that in the developed countries, namely in an environment of scarce resources (technical know-how, human resources, infrastructural facilities, financial resources, policy, general economic environment etc). One can therefore find some characteristics peculiar to small businesses operating in the developing countries (DCs) such as:

- Low initial capital.
- Ownership structure highly family or owner centered.
- Mostly located and managed in private houses.
- Low technology base.
- High labour /turnover ratio.
- High mortality rate.
- Illegal or unregistered operation.
- Low management standard.

The initial capital base of small businesses in the DCs is usually low because of their limited access to source of finance. Possible sources of finance are either internal or external which could come from either the formal or informal sector. The small business's access to the formal sector is usually limited because of a number of requirements which banks have and the small business generally find either very difficult or impossible to meet. From the informal sectors, small businesses have the alternative of either personal savings, borrowing from friends or relatives, credits from a money lender or Small Business Loan Associations or Organisation.

Restriction exists as far as the money lenders are concerned because most of them are so private that they charge very high interest.

The small business Loan Associations and Organisations have also not been very effective as sources of financing for small businesses due to reasons of various kinds. Additionally, the unfavorable economic and social environment of many DCs restricts foreign investments for small business, due to risks which they are exposed to.

The entire above explanations combine to limit the chance of sourcing finance for small businesses and contribute to their low initial capital base.

Due to the limited access to finance from the formal and informal sectors, small businesses have no other alternative than to rely on personal savings of the owners or borrow from friends or relatives to source their initial and working capital. Borrowing from friends or relatives usually does not carry (high) interest or risk, but they are of considerably lower sum when compared to other sources.

The limited access to finance, discussed above also influences the type of small business formed and the organisation structure. Because most of them are financed by either the owners' personal savings or from borrowing from friends, the total control lies always with the owner, who usually sees the enterprise as his personal property.

Most small businesses found in the DCs are located in private houses or personal rooms. This feature is not uncommon with small businesses found in developed countries. What makes it peculiar is that most private houses in DCs have little or no facilities adequate to run a small business efficiently and effectively. There are cases where a small business is located in a semi dilapidated building lacking essential technical and management facilities.

One major characteristic of most small businesses found in the DCs is their low technology base of operations. Unlike their counterparts in developed countries, most small businesses in the DCs are not "modern", meaning that they do not use reasonably up-to-date tools, machinery and equipment or production processes.

Due to low technology base and high population growth rate, which characterizes most DCs, the use of cheap labour is usually dominant in relation to the use of the limited technology.

Although reliable industrial statistics are not available in most DCs due to unreliable data, it could be generally acknowledged that the mortality rate of small businesses found in the DCs is usually very high, considering the type of people who constitute the bulk of the owners and managers of small businesses and the ways in which these small businesses are formed.

In DCs, most small businesses are usually formed by chance or out of want of immediate alternative, often as a result of unemployment or job-frustration. Adequate preparations are not made for their formation and the management is based on trial and error. Added to this is the low level of education of the owners and the lack of necessary experience.

Many small businesses in the DCs also operate illegally or without registration. Either they do so out of ignorance or intentionally, in latter case, to avoid taxes or government regulations. This, including poor databases and inadequate regulatory organs, combine to contribute to inadequate and unreliable data about the number of small business in these countries. For example, a major national survey by the government of India, performed in 1974-75 and aimed at gaining knowledge about the small industries sectors for further planning, found more than half of the small businesses operating in non registered status and about 15% of the registered ones were not traceable.[23] Also recent studies aimed at compilation of data of Asian small businesses lacked reliability due to poor data base (Jones 2012).

Although reliable statistics are not available, it could be considered appropriate to ascertain that many of the small businesses operating in the DCs have standard of labour and management facilities which are very low compared to those in the developed countries. Due to high population rate and low level of economic development, there is consequently abundant unskilled labour in these countries.

Also, due to skill disadvantage in the labour market, this class of labour force usually seeks employment in the small business sector. The poor management facilities which depict the low level of economic and technological development in the DCs add up to reduce the small business management capability and standard.

In conclusion, it can be observed that these peculiar characteristics found in small businesses in the DCs reflect more of their weaknesses than their strengths. These weaknesses have strong negative reflection on the level of their industrial performance and the potential roles which they are expected to play in the overall economy of the DCs. This therefore calls for more attention and more efforts to reduce their weaknesses in order to improve their industrial performance and their aggregate contribution to the overall improvement in the small business sector and economic development of the DCs. Markets are also more broken up into relatively isolated sub markets, because of comparatively inadequate transport and communication. It is also likely there are only few people able to manage large scale industries.

It is important to mention here that some of the factors which enable small businesses to exist, despite the rise of large industries, apply with more force in DCs. The human factor, which weighs on the side of small business, is likely to be even more important in countries that are still in the course of developing modern industry. Therefore, DCs which encourage the development and growth of the small business sector, can expect to take advantages associated with small business development and effective management. As a country moves from a traditional economy through a transitional phase to developing industrialization or modern economy, much effort should be made to improve the efficiency, role and dimension of small businesses, so they can best contribute to industrial development. Though industrialisation does bring large manufacturing units, and though large industries grow relatively to small business, small business will by no means disappear even in highly industrialized countries, but they take more modern forms.

Further reading

Akrasanel N et al, (1983), Rural of Farm Employment in Thailand, BangkoK.

Arief, K. (1992), Small Scale Industries and Small Enterprise Credit Programmes in Indonesia.

Berry, A. (1988), The Relevance of Small Scale Industries New York.

ILO (1986), The Promotion of Small Scale Industries Vol.1.

ILO (2000), Towards Full Employment Production for Columba, ILO

Industrial Policy for Lagos State, Annual Publication of Lagos State Chamber of Commerce and Industries 1970 – 2016.

Industrial Policy of Nigeria: Policy Incentives and Guidelines and Industrial Framework, Publication of the Lagos Chamber of Commerce and Industries 1980 – 2016.

Jones, G. (2012), Small Business Promotion in De4veloping Countries, NY.

CHAPTER 2

RELATIVE SIGNIFICANCE AND POTENTIAL ROLES OF SMALL BUSINESS IN DEVELOPING COUNTRIES (DCS)

Aim

To introduce and explain relative significance of small business in DCs.

Objectives

After studying this chapter you should be able to:

- Understand the small business activities and their relation to the society and economy.
- Understand the significant roles of small business in economy and society of DCs.
- Explain why these roles have continued to increase in recognition.

2.1 Introduction

The preceding chapter has dealt with definitions and characteristics of small business generally, and specifically in DCs.

The reasonable question that would come to mind at this point would definitely be directed towards knowing the reason for the promotion of small business in developing countries. What do these businesses posses to make them real worth adequate attention and promotion?

The increasing interest in the promotion and development of small business could be justified by the relative significance and potential roles they can play in the economic development of any country especially, DCs. These include:

- Employment generation.
- Income distribution.
- Regional distribution of industries and development.
- Linkages.
- Maintaining competition.
- Capital building.
- Production of particular product/market.
- Innovation.
- Savings.
- Improving entrepreneurial roles of women.
- Mobilising indigenous entrepreneurship.

2.2 Employment

The first argument in favor of small business in DCs is their ability to make reasonable contribution to employment generation.

An overwhelming number of reports on small business in recent years continue to highlight the greater labour intensity of this type of business and the importance of channeling a larger share of investment towards them. UNIDO 1993, Weiss, J. (1988, World Assembly of Small Scale Industries, Rabat Symposium on IDDA 1986.World Bank 2011), It is likely that small businesses have less advantage in bargaining supply of machinery than the large ones. As such, there is an incentive for small businesses to invest in a less capital intensive technology because the relative cost difference may be lower.

Today, promoting small business development is seen as a key component of economic development policy. The increasingly important role of small businesses is evident from the extent of self employment through this sector in developed countries, and one of the surest ways of encouraging this employment sector in DCs is to promote small business. In the DCs, the issue of employment is a very sensitive one. Most DCs are faced with a high rate of unemployment, increasing population, limited land availability, and relative shortage of capital and foreign exchange. So concern for job generation often focuses on activities which are lobour intensive.

Based on the above, the promotion and development of small business can help in reducing the rate of unemployment in the developing countries by providing employment opportunity for various categories of the populace -part time, full time employment.

Developing countries generally have been slow to pick up the advantage of small business development and management. However, in the past few years there is evidence of an increasing number of small businesses in these countries, including the relatively increasing share in the number of employment. In Singapore, for example, in 1983, small and medium industries made up over 90% of all enterprises - 50% of the share of employment in Ghana and Pakistan (1984), Ecuador in 1981, and in many other DCs like Niger, Indonesia in 1986, Philippines,

India, Thailand, Republic of South Korea in 1987, Mexico, Columbia, Malaysia and also Brazil in 1987, etc.

A striking feature of small scale manufacturing industries found in both urban and rural DCs is the predominance of small businesses employing less than 10 workers. Data collected by Liedholm and Mead (2000) equally show the bulk of employment provided by these industries.

A feature which has been observed is that employment in this sector is created mainly through an increase in the number of new establishments rather than by growth of existing ones. In addition, with the increase of the number of new establishments, employment in this sector is also experienced to be expanding. This is demonstrated in Kenya, one of the few African countries which maintain a regular statistical series covering small businesses in the formal and informal sectors. Over the period of 1985-1988, employment in small scale manufacturing industries grew at an average rate of 15%.

Majority of manufacturing establishments in the Asian countries comprise small and medium scale industries. They are found to account for over 90% of all the establishments in all Asian countries with exemption of Singapore and Indonesia where they account for 86.7% and 88% respectively. The proportion is even higher in Korea and Japan where nearly all manufacturing enterprises are small and medium scale.

Critique

Due to issues of reliability of data on small business in DCs as hinted earlier in Chapter 1, data to this regard appear to be old and may require cautious handling. However, working on the available data, it could be positively summarized that small businesses have shown some significance in the area of job creation among some DCs reviewed. Nevertheless, the maximum utilization of this potential has not been applied and many DCs are still very far from utilizing this potential efficiently. This is an issue of concern since small business efficient promotion and development would do a lot to reduce the level of unemployment, which characterized the economy of most DCs up date.

It is important to mention here that the attribute of creating job opportunity is not only limited to the small businesses alone, but also obtainable with their larger counterparts. The difference lies in the fact that the additional investment in a small scale industry is usually lower, as small businesses present better opportunities for the use of relatively lobour intensive production techniques. Some challenge this evidence since it is often based on the capital/labour ratio, but the consistency of the finding and the size of the differences revealed, do suggest a true difference.

2.3 Income Distribution

Another argument in favour of small business development and management in DCs is based on the role they can play in income distribution in DCs.

As already explained, many DCs suffer from the problem of unemployment especially, among the abundant unskilled workers who find it difficult to compete in the labour market with the consequence of poverty. The recent surge of interest in small business in the DCs is caused by a heightened awareness among policy makers and international agencies on problems of unemployment and poverty.

By providing employment opportunities for unemployed or under employed, the income level of individuals would be raised and evenly distributed. The main link between encouraging small businesses and reducing poverty and inequality is the increased demand for unskilled labour found abundantly in the rural areas.

2.4 Regional Distribution of Industries and Development

There is a number of attributes that enable small businesses to contribute positively to the regional distribution of industries and industrial development.

As hinted in chapter 1, small businesses are relatively small compared to their larger counterparts and the organisational structure of a small business is usually informal. In most cases, they operate with lower fixed costs, which enable flexibility. Their larger counterparts are usually larger and in most cases operating with a relatively formal organizational structures and with higher fixed cost.

These positive attributes of small business as highlighted above, combine to increase their flexibility and adaptability to changes especially in the local market. In addition the small business can use less complex technology and local raw materials, and since they are not heavily dependent on expensive infrastructure facilities and imported machines, they can be easily established everywhere. Also, the flexible and adaptable nature of small businesses allows them to spring up easily wherever a given opportunity is noticeable. This can lead to an improved interregional job distribution and living standards in these religions.

However, there is a general agreement that the typical industrial growth pattern of many DCs resulted in the urban concentration of few industries existing, at the expense of the rural areas. This trend has been observed in the industrial structure of any DCs with available industries, especially the large scale industries, being sited mostly in the urban area where at least some infrastructure is found. The consequences are strong regional disparities. The promotion of small businesses, especially in the rural areas, would therefore help to reduce these disparities, accelerate rural development and reduce urban migration with the resultant problem of congestion in many DCs.

2.5 Linkages

Apart from regional distribution of industries, the small business can play an important complementary role to large scale industries in the economy of DCs in many ways. They can supply a substantial part of the demand for simple and inexpensive consumer goods at prices within the range of the lower income groups. Specialties that would be uneconomic to be produced by large scale industries are supplied by the small business, and products for which the market is too small to justify mass production can also be made available by the small business.

An important part of emphasis on rural small business is their potential linkage with each other and with other sectors.

Many rural small businesses can cater for the local rural population.

The small business with direct input-output linkage with agriculture may be either agro-oriented or agro based. These can be quite important.

In Pakistan for example, agro oriented small businesses including fertiliser and agricultural implements, accounted for 10% of the total value manufacturing output in 1986-87; and agro-based industries including grain milling, sugar manufacture, leather tanning, cotton textiles, fruit processing, beverage-making, fish processing and tobacco products accounted for some 40% of manufacturing output.

In many other DCs, agro-based industries account for more than 50% of the Manufacturing Value Added (MVA). In some instance (in Nepal) more than three-quarter of MVA is provided by agro-based industries in 2000 (UNDP report 2012).

It should however be added that the input for these industries often have to be imported. The forward linkages are often limited by the low productivity of domestic agriculture.

Agro-oriented industries providing inputs and equipment for agriculture are however of minor importance in many DCs; because of weak demand link (low purchasing power) and lack of domestic known-how. Production is usually restricted to the informal sector (Blacksmith production, hoes etc).

Linkages of industrialisation with other sectors of the economy are critical for promoting small business. This multi-sectoral approach of activities would provide a means to raise the productivity and incomes in all sectors by providing forwards and backward linkage between various markets for goods, services and factors of production.

Small businesses mainly depend on local markets or direct contacts with domestic raw materials. The development of linkages with other domestic sectors would help in reducing some of their constraints (linkage with agriculture, large scale industries, infrastructure etc.).

Linkages are stimulated by economic development and growth in incomes and by development of infrastructure and markets. The less developed an economy, the lower the degree of import linkages due to shortages of foreign exchange and inaccessibility of imported inputs.

Export and import linkages are few in DCs, and when they exist, they are indirect and this can create some advantages for paying attention to sourcing local content. For example in Tanzania some small businesses shifted to manufacturing of wood-based items and in Zambia (North West) the use of iron nails, hinges etc, has been eliminated, minimized or replaced by wooden products used in the manufacturing of furniture due to severe foreign exchange constraints and difficult access to imported inputs. Underdevelopment of trade and communication links between rural and urban areas has also constituted to constraints in linkages for small businesses. Nevertheless, small businesses supply many of larger businesses with parts and components through subcontracting. Subcontracting improves efficiency and reduces production for large scale industries while the small businesses benefits increasing returns of scale by supplying the same number of products to large scale industries. The presence of a well developed pool of small businesses with sub-contracting efforts can serve to stimulate foreign investments.

The development of linkages to large scale industries through sub-contracting or trade usually depends on an expansion of rural markets and of capacities (including engineering skills) of small businesses and on the development of infrastructure like communication networks.

Linkages with large scale industries can be an important source of demand for small business products. Sub-contracting by partner firms to independent small business can play a significant role in several DCs particularly in urban areas. For example, the garment industry in the Philippines, carpet production in Pakistan, and rattan furniture in Indonesia may be cited. This appears to be a quite important mechanism for facilitating the dispersal of suitable industries into the rural areas.

China for example, has gone furthest in organized decentralization of production into the rural industries enterprises where the "head" is located in the city and the "body" in rural areas. Here the urban enterprises provide raw material and product design to rural enterprises within the same sector, while the latter carry out the required processing against a processing fee.

Although it is noticed that linkages with large scale industries through sub-contracting or trade channels to rural areas exist to a limited extent in many DCs, and sub-contracting from large scale industries, where it exists, is usually confined to urban areas like in Tanzania and Zambia.

However, Sri Lanka has developed the "Export Promotion Village" with the objective of increasing export through village-based production linked with large scale industries. India and Pakistan are also countries that show examples of trade and marketing links that extend to rural areas for organizing manufacture, purchase and marketing of handicrafts.

2.6 Maintaining Competition

Small business promotion and establishments can help maintain a competitive atmosphere in any economy in DCs, and help reduce monopolistic tendencies associated with large corporations - as the existence and functioning of a market economy and competition is in many aspects, is due to the existence vast number of small businesses, since they are important sources of intermediate goods for other industries, and they enable the provision of a wider range goods and services in the economy at competitive prices. Small businesses can also help maintain competition in any economic situation, even in a recession, surviving even in any economic situation because of their flexibility and adaptability to business environment. An example is the experience in the Philippines after President Marcos regime and in Singapore, during the recessionary period between 1972 and 1975. Small businesses were found to have contributed significantly to the stabilization of the economy of these countries during these periods.

2.7 Capital Building

Small businesses can help produce reasonable capital building in DCs.

Evidence has shown that the initial capital investments in many small businesses are largely derived from accumulated saving.

This gives incentive for savings and capital building for enterprising, investment, as well as employment opportunity and economic growth in DCs.

It is important that these potentials for capital building in small scales should be utilized in DCs for enterprise development especially, in small business, where capital for starting and running a business generally is very limited.

2.8 Production for a Particular Local Market

Developing countries can also take advantage of small business as they produce for a particular local market.

Small businesses have the advantage of meeting highly specialised or individualized demands.

In addition, they cater for small volumes of a market or one which requires frequent quick adjustments because of the style of changes of particular products or preferences. They also enhance the flexibility and diversification of industrial production because their outlets may be more easily adapted to changing marketing conditions and because they operate profitably even in very narrow markets with low purchasing power.

It is often emphasised that small businesses produce those products which their larger counterparts are not ready to produce mostly because of cost disadvantages. Moreover, small businesses are often associated with relatively simple products to cover local demands especially in consumer goods; they can cater for the poor masses, helping to sustain their basic needs.

The close personal relationship between the owner/manager of a small firm and the people working for him/her can, if properly handled confer a real competitive edge with a particular products or market.

These characteristics could be used efficiently in DCs where the volume of market is small, costs of production is high, local demand for consumer goods is also high and the need to sustain basic needs is prominent.

2.9 Innovation

Small businesses are known to provide many sources of innovations. Many authors wee them as usually more innovative than their larger counterparts because for them, working on new ideas that relate to their profit is motivating factors for innovation a more direct way.

The larger business are seen in many cases or be concentrates on products that have a steady or predictable demand, leaving to small business the slower seller and more risky (pioneer) items. In addition, the large fixed capital of large scale industries does not allow them the flexibility required for innovation. In some cases, only when the small business has already developed a steady market, do large businesses get interested.

Innovation is also seen as key concept of small business entrepreneurial activity since it is widely recognised as crucial factor in successful small business activities in any economy including that of DCs. This advantage can be very useful to the DCs through the innovative small business entrepreneurs that are very much needed in various areas of the economy.

The small business today is seen as playing an important role in the innovation of new products, processes and services in many developed economy. This is based on the advantage of small size that allows flexibility and adaptability and willingness to try new approaches reflecting their opportunist behaviour. The lack of policy and rules in a small, informal structure can also provide a more creative environment than a large hierarchical organisation.

2.10 Savings

The ability to help in mobilizing financial resources is another factor that speaks in favour of the small business.

Their principal source of finance is personal savings, or borrowing from friends or relatives. It is likely that a large proportion of this capital would not have been available from large establishment or to the government for investment.

When spread throughout the economy, this opportunity provided by small business venture can increase the overall savings ratio of population.

This can also help in the use of financial resources which otherwise would have been wasted and also in improving earning opportunities including foreign exchange earnings.

2.11 Improving the Entrepreneurial Role of Women

The growing interest among developed and developing countries in small enterprise creation aimed at women results from the interaction of many important forces.

An increasing number of development economists and policy makers are validating women small enterprise creation as an integral part of local economic development plans because the role of woman in the labour force has dramatically expanded and women are now appearing in every role and occupation including small business enterprises. In addition, policy maker are recognizing that women particularly face unique barrios to achieving their entrepreneurial potential despite all these developments.

To attract resources to venture creation programmes for women, it became necessary to demonstrate that new business creation is a key component of local economic development and that programmes which support women self-employment activities and venture expansion can facilitate business creation.

Women are the primary wage-earners in many developed countries and many women have joined the labour force because of economic necessity. Others have sought to exercise their right to an equal role with men in the economy.

As women presence in the world economy has increased, governmental and intergovernmental units have established advisory bodies to assist improve the status of women to employment opportunities. This effort has however, succeeded in making positive contribution to the status of women, but has not made equal employment a reality. Gaps between male and female pay, employment and occupational status, though shrinking, exist in many developed countries. Nevertheless/ these labour market realities, both positive and negative, play a role in explaining the interest which women exhibit in self-employment and their entrepreneurial potential. The women business owners are increasingly visible in many developed countries.

The rapid rise in the number of women-owned businesses since 1970 represents one of the most significant economic and social developments in the world. New technologies, advances in communication, greater acceptance of working women have created opportunities for women to start their own businesses.

While the growth in the number of women-owned small scale industries in the developed countries is encouraging, the size of such businesses remains small in terms of number of employees.

The European commission study of 17000 women reported in 1987 that more than one half had no employees, one fourth employed salaried workers and 21 per cent employed family members. Similarly, a report from Great Britain indicated 60 percent of women-owned businesses have employees, while only 5 percent have more than 10. Ireland and Germany also indicated that most women-owned ventures have between 1-10 employees. In the U S., Bureau of Census data indicates that in 1982 only 9.8 per cent of women-owned businesses had employees and of these 2.5 per cent more than five. Similarity, a national research study of 468 women businesses found that the majority of the respondents had between 1-10 employees, while 18 percent employed 20 or more full time employees.

The above data indicate the increasing significance of small businesses in improving entrepreneurial talent of women in developed countries.

For the DCs, contribution women entrepreneurs can make to the economic development in the DCs will depend on how much recognition and opportunity is given to them in the area of small business ownership and entrepreneurship. This will give women, who are often socially disadvantaged, an opportunity to wage employment in the small business sector. Engaging in small scale activities also will also provide women with outlets for self fulfillment and personal development, in addition, provide them with a convenient source of income and flexibility in working hours especially for house wives.

By providing employment or remunerative economic activities including supplementing income earned from regular jobs, small businesses women entrepreneurs can improve their earning ability that may also contribute to a reduction of income disparities between men and women.

According to rough estimates produced by research form UNDP/ILO/UNIDO (Jones 2000), small scale industry is a supplementary source of income for an average of over 50% of women engaged in agriculture. Food processing, garments and crafts (including the promotion of basic household items) are among the most common activities. A rural survey of Bagumganj, Bangladesh, (Roger 1988, Thompson 2000) found that women participating in rural industries receive on average an annual income equivalent of US $237,which compared very favorably with a per capital national income in that year (1988). However some women's projects, particularly those of young women, have focused rather on peripheral activities (tie-dye for example) in some African countries. These have often provided quite marginal incomes for a comparatively small group of people.

It's much preferable to adopt programmes and measure which would benefit women in significant numbers and activities. One example of a successful project is that of SEWA, the Self Employed Women's Association in India. The association has organized some 25-35,000 poor urban women in a wide range of occupations as petty vendors and hawkers, labourers, service workers engaged in cleaning and laundry and also home based industries: producing snack foods, garments etc. the association provides certain services such credit, training and assistance in marketing, but also serves to articulate the views of women entrepreneurs as a group. The project thus covers all types of activities. It follows a target group approach, in order to help a particular group of people and in the process renders service to many outside group death.

2.12 Mobilising Indigenous Entrepreneurship

Another argument in favour of small businesses is that they serve as "training grounds" for developing new skills of industrial workers and entrepreneurs.

A small businesses owner is usually described as an entrepreneur because small business triumph and entrepreneurship are closely related. Therefore, entrepreneurship is seen as a key concept associated with small business development and performance. More important is the training and experience which they acquire in the operation of their enterprise s or for working in any. Their role as "incubator" for future Giant Corporation is suited as launching pad for indigenous industrial breakthrough.

In all societies, the traditional industry or sector has preceded the modern ones. There is ample evidence that the latter has evolved through a progressive transformation and modernization of the former. Often critical engines of these changes have been indigenous entrepreneurship, through small business start-ups and development.

In a developing economy such as in the DCs, there is the need for entrepreneurship activities which could take the lead and initiate the highly needed breakthrough in industrialization. Today's turbulent economic climate requires that every one think and act like an entrepreneur. This applies throughout the business world ranging from existing business owner to anyone starting a career in DCs.

Further reading

Child, F. (1990), Small Scale Rural Industry in Kenya, University of California, Los Angeles, African Studies Centre.

Clapham, R.(1985) Small and Medium Enterprise in Southeast Asia, Institute of Southeast Asian Studies Singapore.

Cortes M et al, (1987), Success in Small and Medium Scale Enterprises, The Evidence from Columbia, New York, Oxford University Press

DAC (1991), Development Assistance Committee: Principles for New Orientation in Technical Cooperation.

Dhar, P. (1981), The Role of Small Scale Industries in Indian Economic Development; Institute of Economic Growth, ASIAN Publishing

Gibb, A. (1991), Key Factor of Policy Support for Small Scale and Medium Enterprises, Development Process Gottingen

Geoffrey et al, (1985, 2000), Women in Charge, the experience of the female entrepreneurs, Allen &Urwin, London.

PART 2

THE ENVIRONMENT OF SMALL BUSINESS IN DEVELOPING COUNTRIES (DCS)

INTRODUCTION

This part deals with the environment in terms of policy and institutional framework provided for successful small business development in DCs.

Special attention is being paid to United Nation Industrial Development Organisation (UNIDO) technical assistance to small business in the DCs.

CHAPTER 3

THE POLICY ENVIRONMENT FOR SMALL BUSINESS IN DEVELOPING COUNTRIES (DCS)

Aim

To introduce policy environment of small business in DCs.

Objectives

After studying this chapter you should be able to:

- Understand ppolicy objectives for promoting and developing small business in DCs.
- Understand ppolicy measures to achieve policy objectives for small business development in DCs.

3.1 Introduction

In chapter 2, the significance and potential roles of small business have been reviewed. For the small business to be able to play these roles, a favorable environment, conductive for the growth of small business is very necessary. Small businesses need among others, policy and institutional environments (among others) to help them reduce some competitive disadvantages associated with their characteristics, and such an environment is somewhat lacking in most DCs. This is because in the pursuit of modernization, many DCs are known to have favored establishing large scale businesses to the neglect of small businesses. However, many were faced with sluggish economic growth and very slow expansion of employment in large scale industries.

In response, many DCs have been initiating and implementing a number of policies to improve the environment conducive for small business start-up and development. These policies are as varied as the number of DCs - some countries are very supportive while in others are not. Also, government support for small business in some countries is universal while in others, it is restrictive to certain groups or areas. All the same, it could be said that a policy environment for small business has been somehow noticeable in many DCs. The improvement may also be partly as a reaction to recent changes in the global environment, and the demand for small business development in response. There is a growing interest in small business and entrepreneurship spreading across nations regardless of level of development, resulting in a high level attention been given to small business and entrepreneurship development in DCs. Small business promotion and development is now regarded as a key element in any society and economic development and national governments are finding it very difficult to ignore the impact it has on its society and economic development.

Generally, DCs government policies towards small business promotion are usually expressed in the country's development plans or programmes. In most cases this is formulated under:

- Policy objectives.
- Policy measures.

3.2 Policy Objectives

In many DCs, policy objectives underline the aim behind the promotion of small business, reflecting the role this sector is expected to play.

Although objectives for promoting small business are country specific, a close study of the development plans and programmes of many DCs reveal a similar general characteristic of policy objectives.

This similarity in policy characteristics could be explained, because the DCs appear to have similar economics problems, overpopulation, unemployment, outdated technology, unskilled manpower, area concentration of the few industries, lack of foreign exchange etc. Policy objectives are always directed toward the roles small businesses are to play in solving these problems in DCs.

Efforts to promote small business have some history in the DCs.

In Latin America, organized programmes existed as early as the mid fifties. At that time, technical assistance was still rare, but some financial programmes to promote small business had already been created in Mexico, Venezuela and Argentina, followed by Brazil, Chile and Columbia who launched their own initiative in the sixties.

A remarkable consensus about the objectives and instruments was evident in these early initiatives, which were oriented towards the formation of a layer of modern small scale manufacturing industries to facilitate the transition from household or handicraft enterprises and create the much needed employment.

Developing countries in Asia also appreciated the multiple roles of small business earlier than the DCs in other regions. India for example is one of the earliest countries in the region to express its support for small business. The Indian government policies of protecting and subsidizing small businesses have their genesis in "Gandhian thought", which emphasizes the desirable social and economies consequences of promoting small business.

The "Mahalanobis model" formulated the thinking of Nehru, in which small businesses were viewed primarily as a source of an elastic supply of consumer goods to support the development of the heavy industries. For this reason the Indian government has supported small businesses since the country attained independence in 1947.

Another country is the Philippines, with the record as one of the earliest supporter of small business promotion that could be traced back to the early sixties, articulated fully in the documents entitled "Magna Carta" of social and economic development.

The formulation of policies towards the promotion of small business is somehow late in the African countries when compared with their Asian counterparts. Programmes oriented towards supporting the small business appeared only after independence in the mid and late sixties.

Tanzania and Kenya were among the first to adopt these policies.

The real move towards small scale promotion can be traced to the Industrial Development Decade for Africa and the Lagos Plan of Action in 1986, which was a significant move by African leaders to promote industrial development in their region, especially the development of small business. Before then, just like in many DCs, industrial policy strategy in many African countries has been that of Import Substitution Industrialisation (ISI). This usually centers on large scale and capital intensive industries.

The pre independence era was characterized by the processing of raw materials for export in counties like Cameroon, Ivory Coast, Ghana, Senegal and Nigeria. In former settler's colonies like Kenya and Zimbabwe, as well as in Ghana, Nigeria and Zaire, industrialisation concentrated on the production of bulky low-valued consumer goods.

One effect of the pursuit of the import Substitution Industrialisation strategy has been to produce, in Africa particularly, a bimodal structure in manufacturing with some large modern factories and a vast number of micro enterprises, but very little in between. The phenomenon has been described as the problem of "missing middle".

Apart from a general import substitution policy in many African countries, most of the major policy instruments favour larger industries.

Since the second half of the 80s, there has been a growing awareness of the need to re-orient the basic industrial strategy in many African countries. The large scale industry, being extremely import dependant, has stagnated due to lack of qualified personal and a shortage of foreign exchange to purchase input, spare parts and equipment. By 1983, 23 and in1988, 33 African countries had adopted economic reconstruction policies.

Most countries in Africa have now recognized that small businesses have potentials to contribute significantly to employment, equity, linkages, training, and in alleviating poverty generally. In Kenya for example, the small scale industrial sector is expected to provide 75% of all new jobs created in the urban and 50% of all rural nonfarm employment yearly.

Policy objectives as included in the development plans of many DCs usually focus on the following areas:

- Employment generation.
- Self reliant economy.
- Equity - in opportunity and income distribution.
- Linkages- urban and regional.
- Regional development.
- Entrepreneurship development.

The improvement of the employment situation in the DCs is a major concern and as such, one of the main objective for promoting small business.

As explained earlier, most DCs suffer from a high unemployment rate. Apart from this, most of the few industries are concentrated in some, mostly urban areas. Therefore regional development was highly neglected and linkages did not exist. The notable shortage of capital has reduced the chances of correcting this deficiency.

Fundamentally, the development of a self-reliant economy in DCs requires training programmes that involves the mobilization of human skills and energy. The Lagos Plan of Action stressed that, "since Africa's greatest asset is its human resource, full mobilization and effective utilization of labour force (men, women, youth both trained and untrained) for national development is very essential". There need for equity generation cannot be over-emphasised. For example, women are a distinctive human resource and reproducers of future generations. However, socially defined roles and norms have been found to direct and limit women's incomes generating activities. As industrialisation proceeds, the requirements of women's dual roles increasingly come into conflict. In some cases, a society may value one role more than another. In others, society may through institutional reorganizations, try to reconcile the conflicting duties and demands of these two activities. Therefore, if the industrial development in DCs is to be successfully encouraged through growth of self-reliant economies, it is imperative that planners consider how skills and energies of women can best been integrated into the industrization process particularly in small business sector.

As far as Linkages are concerned, many DCs believe that, small businesses can play an important complementary role to large scale industries in the economy in many ways. They supply a substantial part of the demand for simple and inexpensive consumer goods at prices within the range of the lower income groups.

Small businesses are also expected to play a significant role in entrepreneurship development and regional development in DCs. This is because they possess a number of attributes (small size, flexibility, adaptability, easy to form, etc), that enable them to be a change agent (through creativity and innovation, and contributing positively to the regional distribution of industries and industrial development.

A number of policies have been formulated to drive small business promotion and development agenda in DCs. Some of these are in the areas of:

- ✓ Growth policies.
- ✓ Labour policies/laws.
- ✓ Industrial development policies.
- ✓ Structural adjustment polices.
- ✓ Credit policies.
- ✓ Technical assistance policies.
- ✓ Taxation policies.
- ✓ Regional development policies.
- ✓ Infrastructural development policies.
- ✓ Institutional development policies.
- ✓ Import and export policies, etc.

3.3 Policy Measures

Unlike in the case of policy objectives which revealed similarities among the DCs, there is a vast number of variations in the policy measures and incentives provided for the promotion of these objectives towards small business in the DCs.

The many variations are a result of the different priorities in objectives and the resources available for effective support. However, close study of the development plans and programmes of many DCs reveals the following areas of concentration of policy measures to favour small business:

- Export promotion facilities.
- Products reservation schemes.
- Subcontracting programmes.
- Sales promoting programmes.
- Government buying programmes.
- Training, information, technical services and extension programmes and facilities.
- Financing and credit incentive programmes.
- Common facility programmes.
- Tax incentive programmes.
- Research facilities.
- Institution building and facilities.

Export promotion facilities

Countries which found good opportunities in the export market and which believe to have the corresponding resources needed are seen to take export promotion as their priority objective, and resources therefore are directed to this area. This is the case of Japan, Taiwan, Korea and Pakistan.

In Pakistan for example, small businesses have been designed to be one of the leaders of the export industry. Support therefore constitutes improved design in marketing export facilities.

Products reservation schemes

Products reservation schemes represent a demand side intervention where the available market is specifically set aside for the benefit of the small businesses.

Reservation schemes have not been so common in many DCs, although their use in India for protection and promotion of small business has been extensive and indeed the number of items reserved for small businesses was considerably increased during the second half of the 70s. Recently, there has been discussion about this scheme since it is often questioned whether such a scheme provides competitiveness among small business.

Subcontracting programmes

Another initiative more capable of playing a significant role in dynamic industrial development especially for small business is the encouragement of subcontracting for small businesses.

In the 1980s a number of Export Promotion Villages (EPV) were set up in Sri Lanka with the objective of increasing export through Village based production. The village producers were linked with larger firms operating in the export market, directing some of the expected benefits of an export-oriented economy to the village level. It was also aimed at increasing employment, living standards and entrepreneur ship and productivity.

Sales promotion programmes

Sales promoting especially for rural small businesses has been organized in some DCs as a policy measures in ensuring their efficient development. In the Dhankuta area of Nepal for example, the government has set a Cottage and Handicraft sales promoting scheme. It mainly focuses on the domestic market for traditional textiles.

In some DCs, cooperative sales and marketing organisations are found as well (Sri Lanka, Indonesia).

In African countries, sales promotion is on the whole less developed.

An example is the effort to stimulate traditional industries through a different type of sales promotion in the Salon International de l'Artisant held in Ouagadougou in late 1990.

Government buying programmes

Also, in a number of DCs, the government is an important buyer of small business' product. India provides the most prominent example. Much of the output of the handmade paper industry is purchased and used by government for a variety of special purposes. In Tanzania, government schools purchase only locally made furniture.

In some Asian countries for example, extensive purchasing activities make the government the major or dominant buyer of a wide range of goods and services.

Small business training, information, technical services and extension programmes and facilities

Training, information, technical services and extension services have also been focus point of many DCs. Services in these areas are usually carried out through institutions and centers, meant to serve the small business.

Several types of these institutions and centers have been established in various DCs at different levels. In Nigeria for example, a number of institutions and industrial centers have been established in both the federal and state levels to render these services to small businesses. This is also the case of many other DCs.

Small business financing and credit facilities

Financing and credit facilities for small business has been based on extensive establishment of institutions that are meant to provide financial services and credit facilities to small business in various countries in DCs, for example, through special small business departments in many commercial banks, etc. (more details in the next chapter).

Common facility programmes

Many DCs have Common facility programme designed in various centers and equipped to provide common facilities for small business in many DCs, in such operative activities requiring costly, specialised equipment or special technical knowledge, Such centers also aid in improving techniques, upgrading the quality of finished products, and maintaining standard of quality that can be of great help to small business activities and performance.

Small business tax incentive programmes

Many DCs have introduced and are implementing tax incentive programmes to improve small business operations and competitiveness in the market place, by encouraging established commercial banks as well as establishing industrial development banks to pay special attention to small businesses in their credit facilities programmes, in terms of special small business rates, tax holidays, creation of free zone tax areas, etc.

Technological facilities

Technological facilities from various institutions and centers developed and established in various countries in DCs such as the Industrial Development Centers (IDCs) etc, including international institutions such as UNDO technical assistance facilities have been made available to small business owners for improving their technological programmes, infrastructural facilities and technologies institutions proving technological services to small business. (Details of in the next chapter).

Research facilities

Research facilities such as industrial research centers, raw material research and development councils, industrial research institutes have been established and were made available to small business owners in many DCs (examples in the next chapter).

Further reading

Ho, K (1985), Information Technology Development for Small and Medium Scale Enterprises in Asia and Japan.

Hunt, R. (1987), Small Enterprise Development and the Voluntary Sector, Neck and Nelson Op cit.

ILO, UNIDO, UNDP, the Netherlands (1988), Development of Rural Small Industrial Enterprise, Lesson from Experience.

ILO (2000), Group Based Savings and Credits for Local Poor, ILO, and Geneva.

Nigerian Chamber of Commerce and Industries Reports 1970 – 2016.

Industrial Policy of Nigeria: Policy Incentives and Guidelines and Industrial Framework, Publication of the Lagos Chamber of Commerce and Industries – 1980 – 2016.

OECD (1988), Geographical Distribution of Financial Flows to Developing Countries, Paris.

CHAPTER 4

THE INSTITUTIONAL FRAMEWORK FOR SMALL BUSINESS IN DEVELOPING COUNTRIES (DCS)

Aim

To introduce institutions available for small business promotion in DCs.

Objectives

After studying this chapter you should be able to:

- Identify institutions available for small business development in DCs.
- Explain the significance of these institutions in relation to effective small business development and management.
- Understand weaknesses of these institutions and impact on small business development and management.

4.1 Introduction

In response to the need for an institutional framework that can help translate policies into effective measures and ensure their swift implementation, many DCs have tried to establish appropriate institutions. Government institutions in form of either specialised associations/agencies for small business or multi-purpose institutions have therefore been established. In addition, there are also Non-Governmental Institutions (NGOs) and Associations of Small Businesses.

Areas where these institutions are meant to provide services include:

- Technical and Industrial extension institutions.
- Industrial research institutions.
- Small business financing and credit institutions.
- Common facility centers.
- Small business marketing institutions.
- Small business interest serving organisations.

4.2 Technical and Industrial Advisory/ Extension Institutions

Technical and Industrial Advisory/ Extension Institutions have been developed and established in many DCs to deliver technical advisory/ extension services to small businesses, mainly to help them solve two kinds of problems:

1. Technical production problems - like plant layout and better use of machines and materials.
2. Operations and management problems - involving the choice of product lines in manufacturing, marketing techniques, finance, costing, finance and personal management.

All these problem areas need assistance of trained staff comprising both generalists and specialists. In India, for example, the Ministry of Commerce and Industry, through the Development Commissioner for Small Business, have been operating a national network of small business service institutes and smaller, more specialised industrial extension centers, built up progressively since 1954 and is still expanding, to offer technical and managerial council to individual small business managers, cooperatives, and associations. They also conduct training courses, and prepare and distribute publications on technical production problems and solutions for small units in various lines of industry, and on model schemes for starting new industrial enterprises. Assistance is also given in:

- Obtaining controlled materials.
- Applying for credits and loans through various mechanisms
- Market analysis.
- Obtaining government purchasing contracts.
- Arranging contracts for supply of parts to large firms.

In addition, the Small Industries Development Organisation (SIDO), Small Industries Services Institutes, Extension Centers,

Training and Manufacturing Centers, all offer extension services to small businesses in various areas in India.

Other Technical and Industrial Advisory/ Extension Institutions have been developed and established in many other areas in DCs to deliver technical such as the Small Industries Development Organisation (SIDO) in Tanzania, Management Corporation of the Hong Kong, Nepal Industrial Corporation, Sudan Management Centre.

Major external and advisory assistance to small businesses in Indonesia come from the Small Industrial Development Programmes, Technology Research and Training Programmes of the Ministries of Industry and Manpower. The Small Industry Development Programme provides assistance to cluster of small and medium scale industries. These programmes are mainly carried out by the provincial government and provincial offices of the ministry of industry. The small Industry Development Programme and the Technology and Research Training Programme are directed towards offering advisory and extension services in areas like management training, technology transfer, installation of equipment, etc.

In Malaysia, the Centre for Instructor and Advanced Skill Training offers technical courses to small businesses at very low charges. The Majhis Amarah Rahjat (MARA) enterprises development division also offers extension services in various technical aspects, management, marketing and setting up of small business.

The Industrial Training Institution, the training arm of the ministry of labour in m Malaysia, provides apprenticeship training for small businesses. Also, the Food Technology division of the Malaysia Agricultural Research and Development Institute provides extension training on processing, technology and quality control.

In Senegal, the Ministry of Social Development offers book keeping and organisational building advice as part of its services for a wider promotion of rural women entrepreneurship in food processing co-operatives which also includes technical training and equipment grants.

In Peru the Small Industry Association assists small businesses in normalization procedures and loan applications, offering business assistance and advice in the process.

Similar services are offered by the Association of Columbia Co-operation in Columbia, and the Rural Industrial Programmes in Kenya.

In Liberia, the small business division of the National Investment Commission also offers similar services which have rural as well as urban outreach.

In Philippines, the Medium and Small Industries Co-ordinate Action Programme and Small Business Advisory Centre offer extension and services to small and medium scale industries.

In Pakistan the Small Industries Development Corporation offers assistance on loan application to small businesses. The same is true with small regional offices of the Industries Development Organisation in Tanzania. The Economic and Social Science Education and Extension, an Indonesian Non-Governmental Organisation, also offers help with book keeping and organisational building to rural small scale producers.

4.3 Industrial Research Institutions

Industrial Research Institutions have been developed and established in many DCs to deliver industrial research services that go hand in hand with industrial advisory services. These are needed to identify, carryout and disseminate the result of research effectively and also, to bring industrial problems to the research organisation for solution.

Two kinds of applied industrial research are needed, corresponding to the two areas in which advisory services must give council:

1. Research on technical production problems.
2. Research on problems of operations and business management.

In India, the Development Commissioner for small business and the Small Industries Services Institutes operate an extensive service of economic investigation and information. The results are made available to small industrialists to guide their decisions on expansion of existing industries or establishment of new ones. More than 100 industries outlook reports have been prepared on regional or all-India basis. The reports cover issues on market/ product rate. the prospects of the industry for expansion, and give detailed information, much of it based on field studies with regard to the trends of demand, employment, competition, structure of the industry and main problems.

The Small Industries Services Institutions Thailand, SIDO Tanzania and Kenya, and Industrial Development Centers in various DCs are examples of institutions of this kind that offer similar services to small firms.

4.4 Finance and Credit Service Institutions

Small Business Financing and Credit service Institutions have been developed and established in many DCs to help reduce and possibly eliminate, finance and credit problems which are faced by many small businesses in DCs, and to help existing small firms grow as well as encourage new start –ups.

In Indonesia for example, The Small Enterprises Development Programme, Provincial Projects Development Indonesia, General Rural and Savings Programme, were all established for providing financial assistance to small firms. The Small Enterprises Development Programme provides subsidized credit to indigenous small firms that did not have enough collateral to receive bulk loan on commercial terms. This credit programme which was introduced and co-ordinated by the Bank of Indonesia, (Indonesia Central Bank) was viewed by the Indonesian government as one of the major equity oriented programmes for small businesses. The Small Enterprises Development Programme involves the provision of credit for investment such as in equipment (referred to as "small investment credit) and for permanent working capital (referred to as credit for permanent working capital).

While the bulk of the funds provided for small enterprise programme are provided by the Bank of Indonesia, the programme has also been receiving financial support from the World Bank and the European Community for staff development training and other forms of technical assistance.

The Indonesian Provincial Development Project is aimed at reviving earlier scheme to increase credit facilities to rural small business. A major goal of providing credit to rural small firms is to assist them in the purchase of tools and rural equipment in order to raise the volume and quality of their output. They have also tried to solve the problem of appraising the feasibility of loans to small and medium scale industries by co-operating with the field staff of the ministry of industry.

In the Philippines, the Small and Medium Lending Programme and the Industrial Guarantee and Loan Fund apex of the Bank of Philippines that guarantees fund for small and medium scale industries was established in the same manner with the Provincial Development Project Programme of Indonesia.

General Rural and Saving Association Programmes in many DCs also offer financial assistance to small businesses. Similar assistance from such association is also evident in the Philippines. In Tanzania, rural co-operatives are beginning to be re-established after their destruction in the 70s. In Zambia, there is a strong local rural Credit Union and Saving Association which offers services to farmers as well as to small businesses. In Peru, mention could be made of the Co-operative Credit Centre, a small loan association which makes short loans to individuals primarily for production purpose.

One form of small loan association, or group of savings association which is becoming noticeable in Africa, especially with short term loans for small businesses, is Rotating Savings and Credit Association in West Africa. In it loans are paid to each member in turn, which essentially constitutes a system of pooled savings. This type of association is found in many West African towns and Villages. Credit is being given to members in rotation and also to non members with reasonable interest.

In Malaysia, we have many Small Business Financing and Credit Institutions such as the Malaysia Industrial Development and Finance Berhard (MIDF), Bank of Pembangunam, Malaysia Berhard (BPMB), Bank Kemajuan Pembanguam Malaysia Berhard (BKMB), Majhis Amarah Rahjat (MARA), finance companies, commercial banks, and the World Bank Loan Scheme. The MIDF, BPMB, BKMB, offer long term loans to small business, while short time loans are being offered by MARA, commercial banks and finance companies under the guidelines of the central bank. The central bank requires them to set aside a certain proportion of their loans to small and medium scale industries.

We also have many Small Business Financing and Credit Institutions in the Philippines featuring the Philippines Venture Capital Co-operation (PVCC), Bangong Kilusang Kabuhayn (BKK) and the Philippine National Bank-Small Enterprises Loan Fund (PNB-SELF). These institutions offer special and guaranteed loan funds to small businesses in the Philippines. The commercial and development bank established in various DCs also offer this services.

In Singapore, we also have the Small Industry Finance Scheme, Business Development Scheme, and Business Development Allowance Scheme, targeted towards small businesses. The Small Industry Finance scheme is a low financing scheme for assist small and medium scale industries to upgrade and expand their business opportunities with preference rate involving more than twenty financial institutions. The Business Development Scheme offers grant to encourage small and medium scale industries to develop more business opportunities and identify new niches particularly in international markets. The Liberalized Business Development Allowance Scheme is an allowance of 30% on approved investment machinery which the small firm can offset against its taxable profit.

Small Business Financing and Credit Institutions also exist in Thailand. One of the major small and medium scale industry programmes offered is that provided by the Small Industry Finance Office and the Industrial Finance Corporation of Thailand, primarily established to provide medium and long term soft loans to eligible small and medium scale industries with fixed assets or a particular amount at a point in time.

The Industrial Financial Corporation of Thailand was established to provide management consulting services, mutual funds, provident fund management and leasing to small firms, including loans and equity participation.

4.5 Common Facility Centers

Common Facility Centers have been developed in many DCs to serve the interest of the small firms. These centers have been equipped to perform operative activities requiring costly, specialised equipment or special technical knowledge that can be of great help to small businesses improved management and production techniques, upgrade the quality of their finished products, and sustain required quality standard.

Prominent is the Industrial Estates but a number of small Industries Service Extension Centers also operate common facilities in DCs.

In many DCs, small business factories are often housed in cramped, dark and dirty quarters which are not conducive to good work by human beings or by machines. Improved premises can therefore, stimulate workers and management to better performance and profitability and industrial estates have lately been taken up as an important tool of industrialisation in DCs and can help small businesses in many ways.

Industrial estate can also relieve the small industrialist of the often arduous task of getting title to land, having a building constructed, arranging for electricity connections and the like. This advantage may also be a factor in attracting foreign investment.

The provision of suitable factory premises on rental basis or on hire-purchase helps meet the financial problems of promising small businesses. It is as good as loan, if otherwise the enterprise would have to finance its own building. The risk in this case is comparatively small, because the premises can be rented to some other firms if the first one fails.

An industrial estate can also be used as the focal point for a wide range of other activities to assist small business development. It can provides an excellent location for representatives of advisory and information services, and for research services, financing services, training and other common facilities useful to a group of industrial establishments.

In India, as part of the small industry development programmes, many industrial estates are being built under the second five year plan and more were constructed under preceding development plans.

In Nigeria, Mexico, Brazil, industrial estates have also been established.

Although Industrial Estates have been established in many DCs, there is enough evidence that their use has not been fully maximized due to a number of constraints that surround the running of industrial estate and other problems associated with them.

4.6 Small Business Marketing Institutions

The need for marketing aids for small businesses cannot be over-emphasised, in view of the structural and operational constraints under which they operate.

The small owner/managers generally do not do an adequate job in marketing. This is evident in the market and associated problems faced by small businesses (which will be discussed later), usually structurally distinguishable and therefore, requires specific marketing aids in manufacturing and selling activities.

In response, many DCs have developed and established marketing institutions to provide special marketing aids to small firms.

Marketing aids can take the form of:

- Training on product standardization and quality enforcement.
- Training on attractive packaging and safe transit.
- Advice on the size and variety of products.
- Training in marketing management.
- Training on display techniques.
- Training on negotiating techniques with market dealers.
- Help in the preparation of catalogues.
- Access to participation in trade fairs, etc.

To ensure competitiveness, the product and market oriented aids to small businesses have to be integrated with the economic prospects of small scale products. And a number of DCs have established institutions for marketing assistance to small businesses in their various areas:

For example, SIDO Tanzania, Small Business Corporation in India, Hong Kong Chamber of Commerce and Industries, Tanzania State Handicraft Marketing Company, Punjab Small Industry Corporation in Pakistan, OXFAN in India, all offer marketing advises for a variety of small business.

The Peruvian Small Scale Industry Association organizes common purchasing promoted by the Java Enterprises Development Project.

In Indonesia, the centre for International Trade Exposition Mission (CITEM) organizes export exhibitions.

In Senegal, the SODIZI stimulates groups' purchasing (transport and raw material) by rural small business.

Co-operatives also offer marketing schemes like the Skill Purchasing C-operatives in Haiti, or the Handicrafts Marketing Co-operatives in Kenya.

4.7 Small Business Interest Serving Associations

There are various associations of small business in different countries.

In many DCs, small business association/agencies work under the government ministries, in most cases the Ministry of Industries.

Alternatively there are associations which are quasi government body, such as the Small and Medium Scale Industries Promotion Corporation of the Republic of South Korea.

In the private sector, the various small scale industry organisations are usually established as trade associations or private firms.

The small scale industry trade association may be associated along industrial lines as in the Philippines, or incorporate industries as in Singapore. They may even be organized along provincial lines.

In all cases, they join to form a national association representing all small businesses in the country concerned.

Some are also organized by non-governmental organisations on non-profit basis, such as one organized by the Bali Protestant church in Indonesia.

Encouraging association of entrepreneurs can bring significant advantages, some of which are normally available only to large scale industries. These include trade discounts on purchases of materials, bulk orders from wholesalers or from institutional buyers such as schools, receipt of sub-contracts from large scale industries, collective saving schemes, etc.

The existence of such association is also likely to facilities competence in the apprenticeship scheme which is mostly used by small firms, as they can provide a training environment.

With respect to sub-contracting, it is often suggested that information exchange is likely to be more effectively operated by industry associations than extension agencies. More generally, they could provide articulation of the felt needs of small businesses, negotiating on infrastructure requirements, licensing arrangements and national policy instruments where large scale industries at present have substantial influence.

Some DCs have already moved to this direction to give small business the opportunity to take this advantage. For example, in Peru and Columbia, National Small Industry Association exists. They provide information and sometimes organize common purchases for their member at the same time providing them with the assessments of their business. Also, in the Philippines, small scale associations are mostly chamber of commerce i.e. multi sectoral business associations dominated by land owners and traders. In Zambia small scale industry association exist in Kasur and association of rural working firms in Moshi town. In Rwanda, many grassroots associations had been organized, including Intermediate Trade Federation and a confederation in the capital. They have initiated collective savings scheme to provide credit, set up raw material schemes, and organized training along the lines of established apprenticeship schemes.

In some countries like Indonesia and Singapore, the Government Small Scale Associations are directly involved in the implementation of small scale programmes such as, the director general of small business in Indonesia that plans and implements all the on-going promotion and development programmes for small businesses in the country. Similarly, the Small and Medium Scale Enterprises division in Singapore administers various government assistance programmes for small scale enterprises. In other countries such as Malaysia, the Government Small Scale Agency merely supervises or co-ordinates the function of specialised agencies.

Small business trade associations are also known to try to lobby for the interest of their members as well as providing information and sometimes organize common purchasing for their members. They also strike to assist members with normalization procedures at the same time providing them with assistance in the assessment of their business.

4.8 Institutions And Programmes For Small Business In Nigeria

A number of small business institutions and programmes have been established in Nigeria to facilitate small business promotion in the country. They include:

- Small Business Credit Scheme.
- Industrial Development Centers (IDCs).
- Nigerian Industrial Development Bank (NIDB).
- Nigerian Bank for Commerce and Industry (NBCI).
- Small Business Unit of Central Bank of Nigeria.
- The Working For Yourself Programme (WFYP).
- The Industrial Development Co-ordinating Committee (IDCC).
- The Policy Analysis Department (PAD).
- Industrial Inspectorate Department (IID).
- Industrial Data Bank (IDB).
- Raw Material Research and Development Council (RMRDC).
- Investment Information and Promotion Centre.
- Industrial Training Fund (ITF).
- Standard Organisation of Nigeria (SON).
- Nigerian Employee Consultative Association (NECA).
- Chamber of Commerce and Industries (CCI).
- The Nigerian Economic Reconstruction Fund (NEFUND).
- Industrial Research Institutes.
- SME Equity Investment Scheme.

- **Small Business Credit Scheme**

As explained in the policy objective, the development of small business help create eminent opportunities for existing large workforce, mobilise available local resources, mitigate rural migration and disperse industries within the country.

In an attempt to promote small business, the Nigerian government initiated small business incentive programmes of which the Small Business Credit Scheme is one.

In 1971, the Federal Military Government of Nigeria started to provide a more direct form of financial maintenance to small business. It set up a small scale development programme to provide technical and financial support to small firms. Thereafter, it established the Small Business Credit Scheme to administer small industries credit fund throughout the country.

In the Third national Development Plan 1975 – 1980, the Small Business Credit Fund was formerly launched as the Small Business Credit Scheme. This scheme was a system of matching grants under which each state government sets up credit scheme or fund from which loans are made to small business.

During the period of 1970 – 1974, the financial commitment of the federal state and state government to the scheme was very much established.

In Lagos state, the Small Credit Scheme was set up by the Edict known as Fund law 128 in 1972. The Edict was amended in 1980. The amended legislation stipulates that small businesses are to be assisted not only in cash but also in other ways.

The main objective of the scheme was to provide short-term loans to small businesses in the state who had hitherto been handicapped to raise funds from the commercial banks and other lending institutions because of low credit rating, lack of collateral etc, to encourage dispersal of industries to the rural areas, and to discourage people migration to the urban centers from the rural areas in search of jobs.

The scheme was run by the Ministry of Trade (or Ministry of Commerce and Industry).

The scheme has been assisting small firms in various ways. For example, in procuring raw materials directly from the producers to enable them increase their production capacities and make their products cheaper to buy. The scheme also links small firms to government functionaries for patronage to help in the preparation and payment of contract proceedings or in obtaining import licenses from the government ministry, provide professional advice during regular visits to the sites and arrange seminars for small businesses.

It is important to mention that the scheme has not been as successful as was expected due to mismanagement of funds and many small businesses have failed to pay back loans. Poor recovery of loans has in no doubt reduced the efficiency and effectiveness of the scheme.

- **Industrial Development Centers (IDCs)**

The federal government's active participation in promoting small business in Nigeria is traceable to the setting up of the first Industrial Development Centre (IDC) in Owerri in 1962, by the then Eastern Nigeria Ministry of Trade and Industry, and taken over in 1970 by the federal military government.

Just like many other development centers in many DCs, Nigerian industrial development centers aimed at providing extension services to small businesses, in terms of technical appraisal of loan application, training of entrepreneurs, managerial assistance, product development, production planning and control including other extension services.

In Lagos state, the establishment of an IDC at Imota, in Ikorodu division of Lagos state was completed in 1986. The establishment of the centre is part of the government contribution to the development of small business in the state.

The IDC at Oshogbo was also established and has been playing an active role in the bid to assist and promote small businesses by helping to solve some of their management and related problems, providing seminars, training and consultancy services.

IDCs are not without problems. Because of lack of qualified national staff, they have to rely on foreign experts, who will leave sooner or later, causing hazards with replacements. Apart from this, the centers lack adequate funding for projects. These problems have been evident in the very low number of projects carried out by IDCs therefore, calling for proper attention.

- **Nigerian Industrial Development Bank (NIDB)**

NIDB was set up in 1964, with 59% ownership by the Federal Government and 40% ownership by the the Central Bank of Nigeria. Private Nigerians owned 1%.

The bank is meant to support the small business in form of loan and equities both on medium and long- term basis.

A number of requirements were spelt out which have to be fulfilled before loans can granted. Crucial to this is that the project for which loans are to be sought must be certified to be technically feasible – financially viable and economically desirable. This is an in addition to ensuring that the project promoter is able to contribute their share of 25% of the total project cost.

Potential investors should approach NIDB either through the head office or through its area administration with a formal application which has to be accompanied with feasibility study of the project, certificates of occupancy and incorporation, and three quotations, each for machinery. Preference is given to locally sourced projects.

One of the problems confronting the bank is inadequate funding. The traditional cheap source of funds to development banks is government loans. The funds now appear inadequate because of serious government budgetary and financial constraints. External funds for development bank operations are becoming equally difficult to source because of high level of country's external debts obligations.

Attempts by development banks to raise funds through local capital market are frustrated by the prevailing high interest rate which makes borrowing too expensive for on-lending to special projects assisted by the development banks.

The liquidity position of the development banks is also seriously hampered by a combination of factors such as high exchange rates and high inflation rates. The wide fluctuation in exchange rates has magnified already incurred external loans thus, making repayment difficult. These problems influence the level of their services to small business.

- **Nigerian Bank for Commerce and Industry (NBCI)**

NBCI was set up in 1973 primarily to cater for credit to small and medium businesses.

The Central Bank of Nigeria (CBN) subscribed 40% of the authorized capital of the NBCI. The federal government took up the majority share of 60%.

NBCI is an important instrument for achieving increasing investment growth and development. It provides soft loans through equity participation.

The nature of its operations in the last several years essentially makes it the apex institution of small businesses. Basic loan repayment period is usually 5 years in 20 equal installments, for most projects.

NBCI also grants working capital loans as well as loans for capital intensive projects extending over 10 years. In addition, the bank also administers the Federal Ministry of Industries Special Fund for small business in areas of project appraisal and finance investment supervision, entrepreneurship and self employment, consultation, equipment leasing and syndication.

The NBCI also finances business start-ups and expansion with emphasis on manufacturing oriented small business.

The most outstanding initiative of the bank is the entrepreneurship development programme which is co-sponsored by the Federal Ministry of Industries. NBCI has a division in charge of appraising projects submitted under the entrepreneurship programmes.

- **Small Business Unit of Central Bank of Nigeria**

As a primary organ for projecting and implementing government monetary policies, CBN since 1970 has been instrumental in promoting the development of wholly Nigerian enterprises, particularly in the small business sectors.

To provide a major break- through in the credit delivery for small business, the federal government of Nigeria approached the World Bank for financial assistance to develop a loan project that will complement other financial efforts already going in the country. The loan project is designed to assist the general financial restructuring of industries, help in the re-habilitation and expansion of small businesses, as well as initiating the setting up of new ones.

The Central Bank of Nigeria established the Small and Medium Scale Apex Unit Loan Scheme to administer the credit components and other related activities of the World Bank loans to facilitate project implementation. A project coordinating committee was set up. The Central \bank of Nigeria is expected to lend to eligible participating banks, (commercial banks) meant for final lending to small business. Loans to the participating banks (commercial banks) are at the prevailing re-discount rate. The scheme functions through the commercial banks, which obtain the funds and disburse them to small businesses on a special interest rate.

- **The Working For Yourself Programme (WFYP)**

The Working For Yourself Programme was introduced by the Federal Ministry of Industries, assisted by the International Labour Organisation (ILO), and the British Council.

The WFYP aims at developing entrepreneurial skills and putting innovative ideas to fruition. Under the scheme, a six-week intensive course is conducted at designated centers to train and assist private small business industrialists starting up or funding small businesses.

WFYP are found in many areas of the countries including Akure center and the NBCI is the financial intermediary for the scheme.

Sofar, the programme has been used by many research centers for improvement of small businesses activities. The Centre for Industrial Research and Development has a number of WFYP which have been applied to assist small business activities with assistance from the World Bank.

- **The Industrial Development Co-ordinating Committee (IDCC)**

Initial authorization for establishing new industries was in the past requested from several government ministries. The resulting chaos and delay inevitably slowed down the pace of establishment of new industries including small businesses. Government therefore, established IDCC as a new central agency to oversee required approvals.

The committee comprises the ministries of finance, internal affairs, trade and tourism, science and technology, agriculture, industries, employment, labour and productivity.

The objectives for setting up the committee are to:

- Obviate the delays in granting approval for the establishment of new industries especially for small business.
- Create central approval centers in place of a multitude of them, to avoid unnecessary cost to prospective investors in terms of time and financial resources.
- Remove conflicting and duplicated demands by ministries before approvals are granted.
- Advice on policy review proposals on tariffs, excise duties, various incentive schemes, as they relate to industrial development, especially in the small business industrial sector.
- Ensure adequate co-ordination and objectivity in the nation's industrial development efforts.

The functions of the IDCC are as follows:

- Grant approval for commencement of new businesses and relevant expatriate quotas for them.
- Grant approval for imported capital in new ventures.
- Assistance in procuring machinery and plant equipment plus components.
- Provide engineering design services
- Install plants.

- Commission plants.
- Advise on administration of government industrial incentives.
- Make recommendations on policies including tariff and various measures aimed at ensuring the industrial development of the country.
- Other relevant functions assigned to a committee from time to time to facilitate meaningful industrial development.

Charged with the responsibility of ensuring that all required for the approvals for new businesses, the new arrangement has eliminated the need to obtain the various approvals from different government agencies as previously was the case.

The committee has been undertaking activities in granting the following approvals:

- ✓ Approval status to facilitating capital importation for new venture.
- ✓ Expatriate quotas and business permits.
- ✓ Fiscal concessions on industrial incentives such as pioneer industries, investment in economically disadvantaged areas, export oriented industries, etc.
- ✓ Technology transfer agreements as they relate to assistance in procuring plant, machinery, and components, engineering design series, plant installation, plant commissioning, pre-investment agreements or contracts that is registered under the National Office.

- **The Policy Analysis Department (PAD)**

The government of Nigeria has also established an organ known as the Policy Analysis Department within the Ministry of Industries.

The Policy Analysis Department was set up primarily to undertake the collection of data, conducting of economic research and policy analysis necessary for the evaluation of the effect of industrial policy especially relating to small business.

- **Industrial Inspectorate Department (IID)**

The IID of the Federal Ministry of Industries was set up to play a pivotal role in certifying the actual values of capital investments in building, machinery and equipment of various industries.

It also expected to certify the date of commencement of production for companies that enjoy pioneer status and the value of imported industrial machinery and equipment for the confirmation of the approved status for non- resident capital investment.

The IDD also provides in –house technical services for the ministry including negotiations, equipment selection and implementation of public sector projects. It also plays a key role in the monitoring of Comprehensive Import Supervision Scheme (CISS) to ensure that operations are in the spirit of agreement. The IID also monitors the operations of agents involved in pre-shipment import inspections.

- **Industrial Data Bank (IDB)**

The Industrial Data Bank was established in the Federal Ministries to gather, store and retrieve data.

The data bank provides information on existing industries in various sub-sectors, their production capacities/expansion plants/production costs, the state of the market, price movements, raw materials available in various parts of the country, etc.

A major goal of the data bank is to help provide information for both large and small businesses.

The IDB has not been without problems. Its servicing capacity is very much limited due to lack of funds and adequate data collection aiding facilities. This has affected the quantity and quality of data available to small business. In most cases, data available are not specific to the needs of small business.

- **Raw Material Research and Development Council (RMRDC)**

The RMRDC is a parastatal of the Federal Ministry of Science and Technology.

The council is an umbrella organisation for all the various efforts by public and private sectors in the research and development of local raw materials.

The council works in close collaboration with the Federal Ministry of Industries which has overall responsibility for the development of incentives for local material utilization. Much efforts of the council are centered on small business.

Among others, the RMRDC is involved in:

- Promotion of raw material development and utilization.
- Publicity and commercialization of research findings on local raw material development and utilization.
- Auditing, upgrading and simplifying indigenous technology.
- Promotion of local engineering capability in raw material processing plant design and fabrication.

RMRDC is located in almost all states of the federation including the federal capital territory Abuja. There are also display centers showing available raw materials within the state, products obtainable from raw materials, as well as the technology for processing them, and other investment data.

The aim of display centers include:

- Promotion of awareness of the state's raw material potentials.
- Promotion of the state industrial potentials.
- Stimulating the development of raw materials processing.
- Serving as a resource centre for potential investors.

Setting up raw material display centers involves the collection of data and samples of available materials and their end products. However, many centers need data collection and aiding facilities such as the computer system and function library.

- **Investment Information and Promotion Centre**

In 1966, the federal government of Nigeria launched an Industrial Information and Promotion Centre within the Federal Ministry of Industries.

The principle function of the centre is to promote investment in the industrial sector by providing assistance and information to Nigerians as well as foreign investors.

The centre is meant to guide prospective investors free of charge, on the aspects of their investment proposals.

Since the centre is in close contact with investors and foreign delegations, it is in the position to know their reaction about existing facilities and industrial procedures in Nigeria and get them modified accordingly. It is advisable to contact the Investment Information and Promotion Centre of the Federal Ministry of Industries for the latest information on procedural matters and the industrial climate in Nigeria.

The investment centre in realisation of objectives of industrialisation in Nigeria, participates in trade fairs and exhibitions, sending delegations to other countries and meeting investors and group delegations from abroad.

A number of investors visit the centre daily for information. Most visiting investors want information on two main topics- demand for a particular product and the current production capacity in the country.

Just like the Industrial data Bank, the centre has been having problems acquiring adequate facilities for reliable surveys,

- **Industrial Training Fund (ITF)**

The ITF was established by Decree N0. 47 of 1971, as the body responsible for promoting and encouraging industrial training, and development as well as funding of skills needed to develop and sustain large and small industries in the areas of commerce. In terms of industrial training and development, the ITF is meant to generate indigenous trained manpower sufficient to meet the needs of the economy. To achieve this, the fund provide facilities for training, approve courses and appraise facilities provided for training by other bodies, and regularly considers operational areas of industry and commerce that requires specific manpower training and development.

It also recommends training needed, the standards to be attained, and ensures that such standards are met. In addition ITF assists individual persons or corporate organisations in finding facilities for training for employment in industries and commerce and in the conducting of research into matters relating to training in industry. As of late, ITF has not been very active due to inadequate government funding and support.

- **Standard Organisation of Nigeria (SON)**

The SON is responsible for the standardization and industrial production quality control.

It is meant to prepare standards for products and processes, and ensure compliance with government policy on standardization and quality of products locally manufactured or imported.

It also investigates the quality of products and establishes a quality assurance system including certification of factories, products and laboratories.

The SON maintains reference standards for calibration and verification of measures and measuring instruments, and co-operates with corresponding national and international organisations in relation to securing uniformity in standard specifications.

- **Nigerian Enterprises Promotion Board**

The Nigerian Enterprising Promotion Board was set up by law as an instrument for the implementation of government policies determined to closely involve Nigerians in the industrialisation process.

It acts especially in the small scale industrial sector and intends to promote indigenous enterprises into the commanding heights of the national economy. Under the Nigerian Enterprises Promotion Act, all business enterprises are grouped into schedules. Those classified in Schedule I, are reserved exclusively for Nigerians. They are relatively simple enterprises in terms of technology and capital investment. Foreigners can participate in Schedule II enterprises with up to 90% of equity ownership. It is permissible for companies with a maximum of 60% foreign ownership to invest in or form partnership with Schedule II enterprises (comprising lists of enterprises where foreigners are allowed to participate in terms of ownership and management). The Nigerian Enterprises Promotion Board exists to ensure compliance with these requirements by all business enterprise in the country.

- **Manufacturing Association of Nigeria (MAN)**

The MAN has its members – the national and state large and small scale manufacturing industries.

The main objective of the MAN is to develop and promote the contribution of the manufactures in the national economy through representation of all reputable bodies, government and others whose work may affect directly and indirectly the interest of the manufacturers including small firms. It has representatives in various government organisations for example, the National Economic promotion Council, Export Promotion Council, national Wages Advisory Council and the National Standard organisation.

Through participation in decision making in these organisations, it can exercise a direct influence on industrial policy formation.

The two largest branches of the MAN are located in Apapa and Ikeja in Lagos state.

The association acts as an umbrella for manufacturing organisations of Nigerian and represents the views and interest of the manufacturing sector when dealing with government and other relevant groups.

The MAN collects information and surveys data which is processed and made available to members. It also prepares twice a year, a survey of the manufacturing industry for the cabinet.

- **Nigerian Employee Consultative Association (NECA)**

The main objective of NECA was to provide means for consultations and exchange of information on questions arising from the relation between employers and employees, especially workers in small business sector, where employer-worker relationship is usually poor.

The NECA carries out its own data surveys and analysis, which are then sent to their members.

As one of the central employers' organisation, it represents in similar way to the Manufacturing Organisation of Nigeria, the opinion of the majority of employees vis-à-vis the government.

The NECA is also represented in various government organisations where it can exercise influence.

In addition, it sends delegations on government invitation to ILO conferences. In this way, Nigerian employees are able to express their views on international recommendations which could subsequently become law.

- **Chamber of Commerce and Industries**

The main task of the Chamber of Commerce and Industries is protection of all matters affecting trade and industry for the promotion of the economic growth of the country. There is special interest in small business following the emphasis placed on the need for their development.

The Chamber of Commerce and Industries collects and analyses information, and members of the chamber, which include large, medium and small scale industries is often given information on questions connected to the establishment of new industries, and commercial relations on industrial fairs, customs, tariffs and incentives.

Various chambers are established in all the states of the federation, forming the Nigerian association of Chambers of Commerce and Industries. The association appoints representatives from private sector who are delegated to the government organisation in which the Manufacturing Association of Nigeria and the Nigerian Employee Consultative Association are represented.

The chambers are required to maintain close contact with their ministries.

The Lagos state Chamber of Commerce and Industries is the oldest chamber in Nigeria. Its primary objective is promotion of trade and industry as well as representing the opinion of the business community on matters affecting trade, industry and economy.

- **The Nigerian Economic Reconstruction Fund (NEFUND)**

NERFUND was set up by the Federal Government of Nigeria on January 1989 as a funding mechanism and not a bank. Its aims and objectives are:

- ✓ Correct any observed inadequacy in the provision of medium or long- term financing to small and medium industries, especially manufacturing and agro allied enterprises.
- ✓ Provide medium to long –term loans to participating commercial and merchant banks for lending to small and medium scale industries.
- ✓ Facilitate the provision of loans with 5 – 10 years maturity including a grace period of 1 – 3 years, depending on the nature of the enterprise or project.
- ✓ Provide loans in local and/or foreign currency, depending on the funds available to NERFUND and the project being funded.

In view of the scarcity of foreign exchange for small industries, the NERFUND is expected to enable especially the small business, raise enough money to finance foreign exchange requirements, specifically for importation of machinery, equipment and spare part where possible.

ELIGIBILITY:

- ✓ The enterprise or project is wholly owned by Nigerians.
- ✓ The enterprise or project is small or medium scale by NERFUND and other sources does not exceed a particular amount as specified point in time.
- ✓ The manufacturing project does not use less than 60% locally sourced raw materials.
- ✓ A participating bank has accepted on behalf of the enterprise to assume credit risk.

Once the management of NERFUND is satisfied that the eligibility criteria are met and that an acceptable loan agreement between a small or medium scale enterprise and a participating bank has been drawn up and deposited with NERFUND, funds are released at an agreed intervals following a written request by the participating bank for fund disbursement. Sources of NERFUND funds include the Federal Government of Nigeria, the Central Bank of Nigeria, The African Development Bank, Projected located in rural areas are accorded priority. It is the responsibility of the bank to collect from its customers all interest payments and loan repayments and pay to NERFUND the due amount on or before date.

The central bank is obliged by the Decree setting up NERFUND, to debit the central bank account of the participating banks with the amount due on the loan and credit that amount to the account of NERFUND

Beneficiaries of NERFUND loans are not expected to cover all states of the federation. Interest rates applicable to NERFUND facilities are variable and in particular, will depend on the source of funds at the deposit of NERFUND and are tied to the minimum rediscount rate of the Central bank of Nigeria. The interest rate charged by NERFUND to the participating banks is limited to being 1% above the cost of borrowing the particular fund. Participating banks are allowed a maximum spread of 4% above the interest paid by them to NERFUND.

- **Industrial Research Institutes**

In order to stimulate relevant applied research and development, the federal government of Nigeria established research institutions.

There are many of these research institutions in the country but two of these - Federal Institute of Industrial Research Oshogbo (FIIRO), and the Centre for Industrial Research and Development (CIRD) have been active in fostering research and accomplishing projects toward the promotion and development of small firms.

FIIRO was founded in 1955, following recommendation by the World Bank Mission which visited Nigeria in 1954. Its primary objective is to conduct research on local raw material in order to determine their sustainability for industrial use. The institute is an arm of the Federal Ministry of Industries. FIIRO has been contributing significantly in the area if small business development. Quite a number of small scale projects have gone through the institute. The functions of the institute were being stated as follows:

- ✓ To carry out basic research into raw materials available in Nigeria for the use of the industry and the processes most effectively.
- ✓ To carry out pilot- scale trials of processes found in the laboratory to be technically feasible.
- ✓ To calculate by means of larger scale tests or otherwise, the probable viability of such processes if established on a commercial scale.

The Centre for Industrial Research and Development (CIRD was founded in 1968 as a small research unit of the faculty of social sciences of the University of Ife, to conduct research in small scale business development. It has grown to become autonomous centre with its own facilities. The main areas of activities of the centre include:

- ✓ Entrepreneurship training.
- ✓ Industrial extension services.
- ✓ Management training.

✓ Research and consultancy.

In collaboration with the Durham University Business School, the Federal Ministry of Industries, the Nigerian Bank for Commerce and Industries and some sister institutions, the centre developed a Nigerian model of a Working For Yourself Training Programme. This has been used under the World Bank Scheme for entrepreneurial training in Nigeria. The industrial extension services of the centre include: in- plant consulting, pricing, personnel management and quality control.

- **SME Equity Investment Scheme**

Following the need to improve Equity financing of small businesses in Nigeria, the Small and Medium Enterprises (SME) Equity Investment Scheme was introduced in 1999, a voluntary initiative of the bankers' Committee approved at its 248th meeting held on 21st December 1999.

The initiative was in response to the Federal \government's concerns and policy measures for promoting Small and Medium Enterprises (SME) as vehicles for industrialisation, sustainable economic development, poverty alleviation and employment generation.

To put the scheme in motion, all bankers in Nigeria are required to set aside 10% of their profit- after tax for equity investment and promotion of small and medium scale enterprises as the banking industry contribution to federal government efforts towards stimulating the economic growth, developing local technology, and generating employment.

Every legal small business activity is (exception of trading/ merchandising and financial services) is eligible to receive funding in the form of equity investment or loans at single digit interest rate in order to reduce the burden of interest and other financial charges under normal bank lending, as well as provide financial, advisory, technical and managerial support from the banking industry.

Microfinance enterprises are seen as priority area and ten percent of the funds in the scheme are set aside for lending to them.

Further reading

Harper, M. (1984), Small Business Promotion, Case Studies from Developing Countries, New York.

Industrial Policy of Nigeria: Policy Incentives and Guidelines and Industrial Framework, Publication of the Lagos Chamber of Commerce and Industries – 1980 – 2016.

James Austin (1990), managing in Developing Countries, Strategic Analysis and Operating Techniques.

Lagos State Industrial Guide: Publication of Lagos State Chamber of Commerce and Industries 1992.

Lagos State Progress Report 2000 – 2017.

NIDB; Nigeria, Industrial Development Bank, Annual Report, 2012 -2016.

UNIDO (1991 -2000), Country Brief on Agro-related Metal working

UNIDO (1999), Nigeria Experience on Industrial Project Evaluation, Lagos, Nigeria.

UNIDO, (199 -2011), Nigerian Industrial Research Review Series.

PART 3

MANAGEMENT PROBLEMS OF SMALL BUSINESS IN DEVELOPING COUNTRIES (DCS)

INTRODUCTION

The previous chapters have dealt with the nature of small firms in DCs, their relative significance and the potential roles they can play in an economy. Policies and the institutions existing for the promotion of this sector of industries were also analysed. With these backgrounds context, we can now identify the management problems of small business in DCs.

This part will include chapters 5 and 6 of this book. Chapter 5 will give us an introductory insight into the nature and background of management that will cover necessary areas of management tasks concerned with developing small business in DCs. Chapter 6 will identify sources of management problems challenging the small business performance in DCs.

CHAPTER 5

THE NATURE OF MANAGEMENT

Aim

To introduce the nature of management.

Objectives

After studying this chapter you should be able to:

- Understand basic fundamentals of management.
- Explain the significance of management for successful small business promotion in DCs.

5.1 Introduction

Before going into detail on management problems of small businesses and the many factors that contribute to these problems, an insight into nature of management would help introduce and explain fundamentals of the management as necessary background for better understanding of the management problems of small business in DCs.

The successful development and operation of small firms in DCs requires that they should be managed properly to achieve desired results. Business resources and activities need to be managed -planned, organised, led and controlled so that goals and objectives could be achieved- and as such small businesses need skilled and experienced managers. Since small firms in DCs operate in a developing environment with varied threats and opportunities, the need for efficient and effective management cannot be overemphasised.

5.2 Management Fundamentals

An essential factor that distinguishes all successful organisations whether small or large from unsuccessful ones is management, –evident in the knowledge, skills and experience of managers who run them, reflective on how resources are used effectively, to attain organisational goals and objectives. In other words, these managers understand and are able to apply effectively, basic fundamentals/principles of management to achieve business success. Fundamentals of management could be traced to many management theories, and the development of management and the possibility of a universal definition has been a long and complicated evolutionary process, one that is still under way and is revolutionizing management throughout the world.

Many management theories have been put forward at different era to develop management principles such as - the scientific management approach, the human relation approach, the systems approach, the contingency approach, the modern Management approach, etc.- all aimed at developing management principles and practices for achieving efficiency and effectiveness in organisational performance - whether large or small. The earliest attempt to define and explain what management is and what managers do could be traced back to early management theories or models, especially the classical theorist Henri Fayol. (Fayol 1949), Fayol introduced his understanding of what managers do, by stating what he considered to be the key activities of any industrial undertaken. He outlined six such key activities as follows:

1. Security activities (e.g. safeguarding property).
2. Accounting activities (e.g. providing financial information).
3. Technical activities (e.g. production).
4. Commercial activities (e.g. buying and selling).
5. Financial activities (e.g. securing capital).
6. Management activities (e.g. planning and organising).

According to Fayol, the sixth group of activities in the list required further explanation as the first five activities were already well known.

He suggested that while the other activities were all interdependent to some extent, there was no single one which was concerned with the last group of activities-planning and organising. He therefore isolated the last group of activities which he latter developed and gave the name "management". Fayol defined management as:-"To forecast and plan, to organise, to command and to control". It is interesting to note that his definition of management still remain valid today after many years. Other writers have followed his basic principles with changes of emphases in choices of words rather than principles. For examples, Brech (1957), defined management as –"consisting of planning, control, coordination, motivation". According to Koontz (1984), "management is an operational process best dissected by analysing the managerial function: the five essential managerial functions are planning, organising, staffing, directing and leading and controlling". As much as Fayol's definition has provided the basis for a number of management thoughts, it began to lose touch with the modern society and management as society and business develop and business environment changes rapidly. Many new management theories or models have began to emerge exposing some of the short coming in Fayol's approach or definition of management. His critics have focused on the fact that his definition and some of definitions adapted after him, pay more attention to actions (inputs) of managers, rather than on results (outputs), of managers, and therefore. Only represent the classical approach to management, with less attention to system or contingency approach that considers the business environment as a vital factor. In this regard, Fayol's approach is regarded as being more concerned with efficiency than effectiveness, portraying essentially a leader centred approach to management. This criticism has led to many other writers presenting a more generally acceptable definition of management, examples include Rosemary (1967), who presented a general definition of management, describing a manager as "someone who gets things done through the aid of other people", and Peter Drucker (1999) definition- "management is about getting things done through people and other resources and providing direction and leadership".

In recognition of these facts, management for the purpose of this work is defined as the process of setting and accomplishing goals through the use and co-ordination of human and other related resources within the context of an environment and involves functions like organisation, financing, marketing, production and personnel.

My consideration for this definition is based on the fact that the small business which is the main subject of this work, like other organisations, also has its goals or objectives to achieve. It operates as in an internal environment (which requires application of resources and functional areas based on area functions where small business activities and problems are very prominent), as well as external environment (particularly policy, institutional framework, UNIDO technical assistance as applied to this work), both having strong influences on their management.

5.3 The Small Business Performance in Developing Countries (DCs)

Several efforts in terms of various country-internal policy incentives/ measures and institutions have so far been committed to the promotion of small business in many developing countries (DCs). While all these efforts are commendable, literature reviewed indicate that small businesses are faced with management problems of various kinds considering the low level of their industrial performance.

The performance of small business can be defined in several ways reflecting differences of approach to performance and its measurements. This could include considerations on growth, profitability, market share, independence of firms, and the degree of owner/manager satisfaction with the objectives.

In this book, their general performance and contribution to economic development will be measured mainly by the extent of which their promotional policy objectives are met in DCs. For example, in the case of improving employment opportunity, there has been an increase in the number of new establishment of small businesses, and these new establishments mean new jobs. A problem associated with this is that increase is only found in new establishments but not the already existing ones, and high mortality rates are being reported. Diversification of industries has been very slow, as many rural areas still suffer from industrial drive from rural to urban areas. The high inflation rate in many DCs hardly allows for an improvement in earnings and savings and many DCs still suffer from poverty and hunger etc. All this reflects in many ways the poor performance of the industrial sector, including areas where small businesses are very prominent. A major reason for their poor performance has among other things, has been traced to management problems.These management problems encountered by small firms in DCs contribute directly or indirectly to the sofar poor performance of this business sector to the national economic development of many DCs. In the course of their development in DCs, it becomes very necessary to have current and adequate knowledge of the type of management problems small businesses are facing in DCs so that immediate and appropriate correction and improvements can be made.

Further reading

Harper, M. (1984), Small Business Promotion, Case Studies from Developing Countries, New York.

Industrial Policy of Nigeria: Policy Incentives and Guidelines and Industrial Framework, Publication of the Lagos Chamber of Commerce and Industries – 1980 – 2016.

James Austin (1990), managing in Developing Countries, Strategic Analysis and Operating Techniques

Lagos State Industrial Guide: Publication of Lagos State Chamber of Commerce and Industries 1992.

Lagos State Progress Report 2000 – 2017.

NIDB; Nigeria, Industrial Development Bank, Annual Report, 2012 -2016.

UNIDO (1991 -2000), Country Brief on Agro-related Metal working

UNIDO (1999), Nigeria Experience on Industrial Project Evaluation, Lagos, Nigeria.

UNIDO, (1999 – 2011), Nigerian Industrial Research Review Series.

CHAPTER 6

SOURCES OF MANAGEMENT PROBLEMS OF SMALL BUSINESS IN DEVELOPING COUNTRIES (DCS)

Aim

To introduce and explain sources of management problems of small business in DCs.

Objectives

After studying this chapter you should be able to:

- Identify sources of small business problems in DCs.
- Describe areas identified.
- Explain various factors identified in each area.

6.1 Introduction

As explained earlier, the fundamental difference about managing small business in a developing country is the distinctive developing nature of the business environment- external and internal business environment.

This carries significant managerial implications as external and internal business environment usually affects each other reflecting on the level and quality of small business management task areas - planning and decision making, strategy, leading and controlling as well business functions such as marketing, finance, HRM, operations, etc.

A number of sources of small business management problems have been identified in this book and analysed under the following:

- External environment.
- Internal environment.

6.2 External Environment

6.2.1 Policy Weaknesses

A number of policy weaknesses have been identifies in many DCs that impact on the ability of small firms to manage their business activities to achieve the desired management performance. These include:

- Lack of appropriate policy framework.
- Built-in bias towards large scale industries.
- Lack of private sector participation.
- Lack of balance among the various measures.
- High prices paid for domestic raw materials, no subsides on capital for equipment and low prices for output.
- The effects of the structural adjustment programme.
- Government discrimination.
- Product quality standards.
- Labour policy, bureaucracy, etc.
- Instability.

- **Lack of appropriate policy framework**

In chapter 4 we outlined policy measures tailored to the specific requirement of the sector that are a necessary condition to produce the desired impact. However, DCs in general lack an appropriate policy framework for an effective growth of small business.

Many of the policies on small business in many DCs are fragmented and insufficient. They are neither carefully integrated at the overall level with national development policies, nor at the sectoral level, with industrial development policies.

Strategies and measures are not tailored to the specific needs of the sector. Few countries have as yet well defined a policy framework for effective growth of small firms and where such policies exist, they have been found ineffective due to insufficiently defined target groups, lack of co-ordinated provisions of inputs, as well as legal and procedural barriers. In addition most policy framework for effective growth of small firms has no long term approach in implementation but with frequent interrupting coordination and changes.

- **Built-in bias towards large scale industries**

Although many macro- policies have been identified in DCs, in depth analysis reveals built-in bias towards large scale industries. This is detrimental to the need of small business signaling the need for reforms at the macro- level. In some countries little or no attention has been given to the specific needs and requirements of small firms as it should be. Infrastructure facilities and technical assistance are generally used more by large firms compared to small ones due to their advantage in terms of policy favour.

- **Lack of private sector participation**

It is also discouraging to notice that very few small business policies in DCs encourage private sector participation in small business development.

The governments in many DCs seem to think they know what is best for small business and that the private sector has little to contribute.

As a result the private sector is not usually represented in many small business advisory or policy formulation bodies, and small business agencies are predominantly if not wholly, controlled by government representatives.

- **Lack of balance among the various measures**

Although there is a variety of policy measures' supporting small business in the DCs, there is lack of balance among the various measures in various countries. This does not call for a mere combination of policies in paper but requires an adequate implementation.

Briefly, small scale policy measures may be grouped in three categories, namely: those which are stimulatory, supportive and sustaining:

- ✓ Stimulatory measures are those which stimulate entrepreneurship. Supportive measures help small business to establish and run their enterprise probably comprising financial, marketing and technological assistance etc.
- ✓ Sustaining measures ensure the continued efficiency and profitable functioning of small business, and include measures relating to modernization and expansion.

Effective realisation of small business potential requires a combination of stimulating supportive and sustaining policies which take care of the demand and the supply side effect of these policies. However, analysis of small business policy measures in various DCs reveal that many of them are focused on supportive activities especially in financial support. This is the case in many Asian countries.

Additionally, the support measures exhibit deficiencies. While in theory some of these benefits may be available to small business, in practice they remain beyond their grasp. For example, credits from bank do not reach the small business because of their smaller sizes of loan, inefficient collateral's and high administrative cost of such loans to banks. In the Philippines, evidence has been found of high effective rate of tariff protection of 25-205% for large business sector where large enterprises predominate compared to negative rates for small business sector which provides two third of small scale employment. Indonesia has a similar negative correlation of the effective protection rate.

- **High prices paid for domestic inputs**

Weaknesses in policies in DCs have left many small firms in DC with no choice but to pay high prices for domestic raw materials, with no subsides on imported capital equipment.

For example, study sponsored by the World Bank and the government of Tanzania concluded that small businesses have been penalized through lower import content, high foreign exchange rate resulting to high prices paid for imported materials and capital equipment.

- **The effects of the structural adjustment policy**

Structural Adjustment Programme introduced by many countries in DCs has encouraged the introduction of of liberalization imports in these countries and this has produced mixed results for small firms in many DCs.

Liberalization has meant absence of attention to problems of small business, and competition for cheaper imports or large scale manufactured goods has adversely affected existing small business.

The demand push from liberalization provided incentives to certain small business but affected others adversely depending on each country's situation.

Among the countries which adopted liberalization measure, Sri Lanka has the longest experience. Liberalized import of finished goods or products into the country has led to dumping and below-cost prices small business had to compete with. It has also shifted demand for domestic goods to imported products.

Liberated imports of raw materials and capital equipment have benefited the large scale industries who took the advantage of economies of scale by expanding their production and buying raw materials in bulk. Small businesses were discriminated in various ways by commercial banks and hence they could not benefit from the increased financial resources mobilization.

- **Government discrimination**

Generally government policies, regulations and practices in many DCs do not deliberately discriminate small business. Nevertheless, the nature of these policies and regulations and the way they are implemented often impose penalties to small businesses. This is true for a wide variety of trade and investment promotion policies as well as some monetary and credit policies which are applied in many DCs.

In the meantime small businesses in many DCs continue to suffer from the unintended bias of various forms of government policies.

A comparison of the structure of effective protective rates and the size distribution of establishment in the Asian countries reveals that effective protection tends to be particularly high in industries where small businesses share in production are relatively low. This finding also shows that the structure of effective protection in Asian countries except for Singapore is bias against not only certain industries, but also against small businesses within individual industries. In most cases, the present system of protection is not reflection of deliberated policies in accordance with clear objectives.

Due to their relative importance and better access to influential administrators, large businesses are likely to be more successful than small businesses in arranging government protection against external competition. Since protection is granted against imports of specific products, and since manufacturing industries produce a number of different products, large industries may be able to arrange protection but small businesses in the same industry may not, as large and small firms differ with respect to their production mix.

In the case of providing fiscal incentives to encourage the development of the industry, a striking feature of the fiscal inceptive system in many Asian countries is the attempt to link the value of such incentives to the level of investment. This implies that large enterprises in terms of investment would receive greater benefits.

Another form of discrimination against small firms in DCs relates to the other activities of the state. In some Asian countries for example, extensive purchasing activities make the government the major or dominant buyer of a wide range of goods and services. Government purchasing activities inevitably discriminate small firms even when not intended. Generally, in the interest of administrative efficiency, and in the search for economies in purchasing, government purchasing agencies tend to place their orders in relatively large amounts at a time and often by selective tenders. Bulk purchasing and selective tenders tend to favour the larger enterprises, so small firms are generally left out of the lucrative government purchasing business. Such a case is found in India.

Other forms of discrimination are less subtle but not less effective. Consider for example, government regulations which prescribe zoning regulations. These regulations have most severe impact on small business because of their inadequate capital and the limited geographic nature of their markets. Due to inadequate capital, a number of small businesses often first set up shop in residential areas. Initially local authorities tolerated their existence but subsequently, regulations are tightened up and more strictly enforced. At the same time the local authorities failed to appreciate the location problems of firms and do not provide alternate sites before evicting these enterprises. As a result, a number of small firms particularly in the larger towns in some of the Asian countries have seen their business disrupted and in some cases have been forced to close their shop.

- **Indiscriminate product quality standards**

Another regulation which has adverse effect on small business promotion is that relating to product quality standards.

Product quality standard requirements are imposed indiscriminately in many DCs in relation to small business products and services.

It is clear that product standards requirement is a necessary in DCs and such standards requirement may be relevant to an export oriented small business meet up with international completion, but when applied indiscriminately to goods meant for local consumption, they impose a heavy burden on small business development in DCs, for example those introduced in the Malaysian Pineapple Canning Industry were found to have discouraged the entry of small less capital intensive enterprise into the industry.

- **Labour policy, bureaucracy, etc**

Many governments in DCs have formulated and implemented their policies on small business without careful assessment and analysis of the impact on small business activities and performance. On such policy is the labour policy. A study in the Philippines found that about one third of total number of small scale entrepreneurs view certain policies as adversely affecting their business. The policies most mentioned were labour policy, especially the minimum wage law - the requirement for thirteen months pay, and social security benefits. The bureaucratic papers required in securing licenses, registrations and permits were also deplored by many as hampering business transactions. Among the other unpopular policies were: high sales and manufacturer taxes, high tariff duties for importation of raw materials, environmental protection policies (like restriction on cutting down trees), zoning requirements, credit policies etc. For the small business, these policies affect their business adversely by reducing their profit margin and competitive strengths through increase in costs.

- **Instability**

Instability in policies and government is also another point.

It is not only the economic environment alone but the general socio-economic and political environment which stimulates or hampers potential entrepreneurs to risk their funds and invest in their own enterprises.

In cases of economies instability and uncertainty, entrepreneurs would not invest in small business even if there were a network of promotional measures available.

6.2.2 Institutional Weaknesses

Institutions meant to serve small businesses in DCs also have weaknesses that directly or indirectly affect their ability to serve the small business effectively and reflecting in their management performance. They are traced to:

- Few private sector small business institutions.
- Public sector control of small business institutions.
- Overshadowed by the public sector.
- Absence of strong small business representatives.
- Poor staffing and performance.
- Poor salaries.
- Organisational problems.
- Few special small business institutions.
- Inadequate location.
- Fake institutions.
- Multiple services.

- **Few private sector small business institutions**

There are very few private sector small business institutions in most DCs, which are involved in one way or other with small business development. For example, here is hardly any small business agency in the private sector worthy of mentioning and where they exist, their membership is largely restricted, and they are often being overshadowed by the public sector. Often, there is no co-ordination or consultation between the public and private sector small scale industrial institutions. Both parties in most cases function in isolation.

Usually, the government does not see any need in co-operating with the private institutions either in planning or in the implementation of small scale projects and programmes. This means that in most cases the views and programmes of the small business agencies in private sectors are usually not considered, although this sector is bound to be in a better position to know and satisfy the needed of small business.

- **Public sector control of small business institutions**

Since there are few private sector small business institutions, most of the institutions established to render services to small businesses in most DCs are public sector oriented and under government control.

This public control of small business institution has been found to have constituted to the poor performance of many small business institutions under government control. Numerous failures of public institutions have been traced to this fact. For example, SIDO in Tanzania, BIPIK in Indonesia, are all in public sector small business institutions and in public control and these institutions have common performance inadequacies. The SIDO in Tanzania has not been able to supply rural blacksmiths efficiently with steel, BIPIK in Indonesia, also finds it hard to provide raw materials to bamboo weavers. All their operations have been found to be very costly with high overhead and bureaucratic procedures and lacking adequate and needed governmental financial assistance.

Also, most public owned production centers in DCs generally do not have impressive production records. Evidence shows that they usually exhibit lower production than their private sector counterparts. They are sluggishly run, over endowed with relatively capital intensive equipment beyond the means of small businesses and provide no useful demonstration examples to small business.

- **Absence of small business strong representatives**

Many small business institutions are found to run with absence of strong small business representatives.

In absence of strong representatives, the view of small businesses especially in relation to their needs and problems are seldom represented directly to government.

Decisions concerning the welfare of small business are often passed on to them indirectly and eventually become interpreted or distorted. This of course affects the type of assistance provided to small business.

- **Poor management in some institutions,**

A major weakness of some small business institutions in DCs is traced to poor management in some institutions, and in many cases theory differs from practices. For example, a number of small business institutions set up to render financial assistance to small businesses have shown weaknesses in their financial programmes for small business.

In Malaysia, although the General Guarantee Scheme (GGS) and the Special Loan Scheme (SLS) allowed Bumiputra people to borrow up to M$2,000,000 in 1984 and 1987, there were no loans approved under the SLS and only 18 loans under the GGS for amounts ranging only from M$50.000- M$200.000.

- **Poor staffing and performance**

Poor staffing is another weakness that has led to poor performance of many small business institutions and their inability to produce required services to their clients. For example, there is evidence that most of the staffing in the public small business institutions is somehow manipulated and based on favour instead of competence, resulting to poor staffing of many institutions. In addition there are a number of disappointments with the attitude to work of the staff that usually see the institution as government property that has not much to do with them, reflecting in poor service and performance delivering in relation to the needs of small firms. Since there is no correlation between their performance and their wages, performance is low. Sometimes, there are possibilities that the participants skin funds to their private benefits, but to the detriment of the institution and small business expectations. Training facilities are sometimes seriously under-utilised because of lack of adequate technical training staff or the nonchalant attitude of staff and trainees.

- **Poor salaries**

Poor salaries paid to workers in public sector small business institution is something that is recognized in DCs.

There is the problem of poor/low salaries not adequate to attract the outstanding individuals needed for all positions.

In addition, government administrative restrictions designed for control rather than for development do not provide the opportunity for recognizing or giving incentives for superior performance.

- **Organisational problems**

Many small business institutions in DCs especially, the multipurpose institutions also run into organisational problems. Sometimes, these institutions get blocked from their multifarious function and become departmentalized along the line causing bureaucratic hazards. In many cases, their comprehensive packages are not delivered and when, there is the problem of conflicting interests of multiple functions. Then, the institutions runs the risk of mis-budgeting the various functions, over-emphasizing some at the expense of others, dampening the activities of small business. For example, many small businesses receive training from SIDO in Pejub, Tanzania and Indonesia but they do not receive equipment loans or effective marketing assistance. On the other hand, some receive equipment but do not receive training as is the case with many recipients of SIDO hire purchase in Tanzania.

- **Very few special small business institutions**

In some DCs, (unlike in Nigeria, India, etc) there are very few special small business institutions. This raises the problem of availability of enough special small scale institutions to serve the needs of the small business.

The situation is that majority of small business institutions are multi-purpose functional institutions serving both the small scale institutions and their larger counterparts. In many cases, this gives room for discrimination against small business, since these institutions for many reasons prefer to render most of their services to the larger ones.

- **Inadequate location**

Many small business institutions are found to be inadequately located

Inadequate location of some of these institutions contributes to poor performance on both sides i.e., the small business and the institutions themselves. Sometimes they are located in areas very far from reach of their clients which they are meant to serve.

Poor transportation and communication systems increase the extent of the problems involved. In addition, most institutions in the DCs are urban based with the disadvantage on rural areas. Their urban base generally stuns their effectiveness for rural small business. For example, in Zambia, SIDO does little outside the main towns and whereas Village Industry Services (VIS) is not actively rural, many of its activities are in support of small industries in Lusaka.

In Tanzania, SIDO's loans and extension services are overwhelmingly concentrated in Dar-EL Salaam and regional centers.

In Indonesia, the bulk of the BIPIK funds have gone to the provision of industrial estate mostly in large city areas. The same is the case of Sind Industrial Corporation in Pakistan.

For the industrial estates, a number of them have failed to meet up with the services they are expected to provide. Most of them usually fail to secure a good location. Many of them are found located several kilometers away from the town they serve. Often their locations are determined politically not economically.

In Pakistan for example, many estates are located kilometers from the town they serve and this alone make it difficult for them to attain their clients and also for the clients reaching them.

Desk studies reveal cases of problems in acquisition of land in Nepal, Pakistan, Peru etc. Replacement capital is often eroded due to continue leasing at uneconomic or subsidized rents to fortunate occupants. Obtaining permits and approvals take a lot of time.

- **Fake institutions**

Another important problem faced by small businesses as regards the institutions serving them is the problem of "fake institutions".

There are instances of fake institutions in some DCs which are not operating really to render services to SSIs, but were set up in order to attract cheap credit or other benefits from the authorities.

A number of them operate with fake identities in many DCs up till date.

Some Non Governmental Organisations (NGOs) have been over-emphasizing the welfare concern and under emphasizing input and upgrading. These NGOs seem to be concentrating on "groups" to attract attention and assistance, rather than "potentials".

- **Multiple services**

There are also cases where institutions attempts to provide as many services as possible to as many small businesses as could be reached.

The quality and impact of their services have been less satisfactory.

An example of this is the CSIO technical assistance in India where attempts have been made to provide too many services to too many locations for their available resources of trained manpower and equipment. Concentrations of activity in major locations and for those industries where maximum contribution can be made to a rational growth objective were neglected. Another good example is SIDO Tanzania.

6.2.3 Infrastructure

Another external environmental factor that contributes to management problems of small business in DCs is inadequate infrastructural facilities, well documented in the literature.

Inadequacies in physical and social infrastructure exist in:

- Road network.
- Electricity supply.
- Water supply.
- Communication.
- Social amenities, etc.

Inadequate existence of essential services, such as access to good roads, telecommunication, electricity and water supply constrain the operational performance of any business large or small. This is the case with small businesses in many DCs, most of which cannot afford alternatives by themselves.

Electricity is needed to increase viability in work places and to produce the mechanical power for machinery.

Water is needed for cleaning mixing cooling and for domestic use of the labour force. The role of time and communication in the success of any business cannot be overemphasized; therefore efficient telecommunication is highly needed. Good roads and railways, air and marine transportation systems are required for efficient distribution of goods, the enlargement of markets and the purchase of materials for inputs.

In the DCs, this physical infrastructure is still very scarce. Railways are often nonexistent or useless. The road network, as the main means of transportation, is still in its infancy. Well over half of the total road mileages in most DCs are not tarred, and only about half of the roads are motorable. During the rainy season large parts of the states, especially in the rural areas, remain isolated, even when served by roads. For most parts, road transportation is uncertain, tedious and costly.

Electricity is available only in few areas and usually very inefficient. Power failures and disruptions are a common factor in many DCs. This usually disturbs production processes at factories thereby, wasting thousands of man hours and other resources. This inefficiency of power supply can also cause damages to plants and machines. All this combines to inflate the cost of production. While tap water is available in the cities, there is an acute shortage in the rural areas. The development of telecommunication in many DCs is still in its beginning, although there is a resent improvement in some DCs. The inadequate provision of telecommunication facilities would not matter much if there were quick efficient means of transportation.

As it is, the restricted facilities for travelling have to be compensated by contacting business partners and customers via telephones and letters. In principle, it is possible for industries to construct or buy some infrastructure facilities they need, in order to avoid some of these constraints. Where there is no electricity, an enterprise could install its own power generator. The truth is that small businesses are handicapped in taking this alternative because of their restricted financial position and even if they manage to adjust in this area, their competitive strength is usually affected through high operating cost. This in turn affects their product prices and hence the demand for these products.

In most DCs, small businesses have a narrow choice of sites and premises for their operations due to shortages of capital. Very often, they begin production in a small building or a part of a building which in many cases may also serve as residence. Initially, this arrangement may be tolerated but as the town expands and develops, zoning regulations may force him to move out. In any case, most SSIs are located in places which are not suitable for industrial purposes. This situation raises some grave problems relating to infrastructure and socio-economies consideration, both for the enterprise itself and for residential areas in form of noises, dirt, refuse and the risk, not to mention other problems such as traffic and traffic congestion's. For example 40% of the 499 entrepreneurs surveyed in Butterworth, Malaysia in 20011 had no waste containers. 64 out of 191 enterprises burned their waste and a further 8% just dumped their waste. Relocation of small business is not easy because in some countries, the government often fails to make provision for the small business in planning industrials estates. Take as an example the State Economic Development Corporation of Malaysia (SEDC) which has so far completely excluded from its planning (e.g., in plot delineation and rents) the possibility of allocation of industrial premises to small businesses on a rental basis or purchase by installment. In the case of Indonesia, although small businesses were officially given priority for moving into the first two industrial zones opened in Indonesia at the beginning of the 1970s (Jakarta, Surabaya), it's the large and medium firms that have made much greater use of this opportunity. Also even in countries where industrial estates are available, the cost might deter the small business. In most cases the industrial estates usually lack almost all the facilities which it is meant to provide. For the industrial estates, a number of them have failed to meet up with the services they are expected to provide. Lack of adequate facilities is the major reason for this. Provision of facilities is not particularly efficient as many lack needed common facilities. If available, common facilities derive their business mainly from the larger industries. There is little evidence that industrial estates stimulate demand and industrial development. SIDO Tanzania found out that its most successful clients are found in smaller towns and not in the industrial estate.

6.3 Internal Environment

6.3.1 Finance

Because of many reasons, small businesses in DCs have a number of problems with financing their ventures.

Generally, the sources of capital for small businesses in DCs are usually through:

- Personal savings.
- Friend or relative.
- Money lenders.
- Financing institutions.
- Small and medium industries development associations.
- Savings and loan organisations.

A major means of souring financing is credit from financial institutions, especially from commercial banks. Small firms in DCs are however having problems in obtaining credit from a financial institution, especially the commercial banks.

On the supply side, there are several reasons why commercial banks are reluctant to lend to the small businesses in DCs.

The banks consider it less profitable to lend to the small business because of high administrative lending costs with small credits and greater risks. The strong impact of administrative costs does not only affect the profitability of the loan scheme to small business but the entire profitability of bank loans.

Screening contracts are subject to significant economic of scale. Large loans are cheaper per unit cost to develop, appraise, disburse, supervise and collect. Also most small businesses are not able to provide the collateral's demanded by banks for lending. The risk of business failure is higher for small business and many of them do not have proper record keeping.

A good record system is useful for every organisation, small or big. Records provide most of the information decision makers need to support their analysis and resolve issues, and since decision makers who manage with information are more efficient and effective than those who do not, good record keeping is a necessity for a business that wishes to survive. The primary role of good accounting and book keeping in the credit system is to establish a basis for confidence and trust. However, many small businesses in the DCs are unable to keep proper accounting records or other documentation called for by the banks. In most cases such records do not exist, making approval of loans difficult and cumbersome.

A common problem with many small business loans proposals is that many documents presented are not genuine, inadequate or improper. In an attempt to paint a rosy picture so as to get the loan, costs are underestimated so that even if the small business owner is lucky enough to get the loan, more often than not, it fails to propel the loan project to the operational stage and the enterprise has to struggle in search of funds, meanwhile interest charges have begun to mount and if eventually funds are not forth coming, the project might not reach the take off and the enterprise finds itself in debt.

In a study of small business in Malaysia (Jones 2009), it was found that most of the firms surveyed kept not detailed account. Another study in Korea (Johnson 2010), reports that fewer than one half of small businesses studied have any recognizable form of book keeping at all, and similar results have been found in the Philippines. There are even cases where loans were given but they were treated as private property for immediate private consumption (Johnson 2011).

Financial institutions in the DCs are especially handicapped when they seek to reduce the risk of failure through an intensive contact with small businesses. Weak transport and communication facilities in many DCs make it more difficult to keep in touch with small business credit-takers. This results in an unclear picture of the economic and management situation of small business as borrowers and would-be borrowers, making credit less likely and reduces the amount of pressure that can be exerted on them to keep them on their promises, and expected performance level.

On the demand side, there is reluctance from many small businesses to obtaining loans from banks. The administrative requirements and formalities to acquire the loan, particularly the time and paper work involved, are practical obstacles, usually leading to delays and untimely disbursement of approved loans with the resultant effect of inadequate implementation of funded projects.

In Asian countries for example, it has been discovered that many small businesses never approach a bank when they are short of funds because they do not think they can get a bank loan. In fact a number of small businesses that tried to obtain assistance from the commercial banks have been turned away, fulfilling their preconception.

A Bank of Thailand survey (Johnson 2010), found that small and medium scale industries required a total credit of about 10,000 million (baht) a year, but the government and organized financial institutions could only provide 5 to 10 percent of the required amount. The reminder had to be obtained from non institutional sources at a very high rate of interest. Another similar study in Malaysia estimated that small and medium scale industries required banks loans valued at M$54,800 million but received less than M$300 million.

As a result of the various risks associated with small business lending, Banks have resorted to demanding stiff collateral security for the loans to this sector as a guarantee against recovery in case of failures to pay back the loans.

The stiff collateral security requirement demanded by banks is often impossible for the small business to provide, so they lose their chance of obtaining loans. The banks have to charge higher interest rate on loans to the small business in relation to their larger counterpart, in line with security requirement and their inability to provide them increases the risk or lending. The high interest rates charged on a loan have also scared off many existing and potential small business from approaching the established banks for loans.

The attitude of bank officials is also a critical factor. In DCs, it is alleged that the bank manager considers him/herself as a member of a different social class and often tends to treat the poorly educated small business borrowers with caution.

The idea of individualism and lack of trust among small scale industrialists also contributes to their financial problems. As a result of wanting to do everything alone, their chances and ability to attract funds or resources are limited. This makes them fall to professional money lenders of the informal financing sectors who charge very high rates of interest. Consequently, many small businesses try to minimize their loan volume from informal sources by keeping low stocks of working capital. Inputs are then purchased from sales received liquidity which renders them more vulnerable to market fluctuations.

Other source of credit for small businesses in DCs includes unlicensed money lenders, saving and loan associations and the Small Medium Scale Industries Associations. Obviously, souring finance from the money lenders involves a great risk. Many of these sources are operated illegally and there have been several cases where the organizers of mutual credit associations have disappeared with funds.

In view of the above, it is not surprising that lack of credit from financial institutions has been identified as one of the major factors inhibiting the expansion of small business in many developing countries.

Financial programmes initiated by Small Medium Scale Industries Associations (SMIDAs) offer another source of financing for small business. These are generally initiated by SMIDAs, dissatisfied with the banks' lending performance to small business. In Tanzania for example, SIDO has managed a low interest-rate equipment hire-purchase loan scheme for small businesses. The equipment is procured centrally by Small Industries Development Organisation (SIDO) headquarters.

This has been set up to solve the frequently delays and inappropriate equipment facilities in small business. The programmes have not been found functionally viable or expanding.

In Kenya, the Kenyan industrial estate operates a programme of small loans to small business although, with mixed feelings.

The experience in Indonesia has not been better. There, the agency chooses the types and recipients of loans, while leaving the disbursement and collection to a bank. The problem is usually that apart from the lack of adequate knowledge of borrowers' creditworthiness, which was not determined solely, or not at all by the banks, the banks were not in control of the programmes and felt absolved of the responsibility for the financial success. The result has been a high incident of bad debts and financial non sustainability. They usually run down without achieving a long term, wide spread impact. Such programmes can therefore not be regarded as generally effective for small scale promotion. The reason is probably that they have regarded their clients as favored group without much regard to their credit worthiness. Since they have also been based on "outside" government external support or funds, both the programmes organizer and their clients have tended to regard the loans as something of a gift. The experience of the Bangladesh Small Industries Credit in Bangladesh shows similar result (Baron 2010).

Saving and loans organisations (SLAs) also exist in some DCs as a source of finance for small business.

In Zambia for example, there is a strong system of local rural credit union and savings associations, (CUSAS).

There is a similar strong small scale savings and loan association, the Co-operative Credit Scheme in Peru, which makes short term loans to individuals for industrial purposes in any productive sector including trade and services. The BRIs new programme in Indonesia is run on similar principles although being managed by banks. There are also numerous programmes of this sort set up in various DCs, especially by the Non-Governmental Associations (NGOs).

It seems that the small savings and loan associations have been able to prosper in both rural and urban small business. The loans are disbursed quicker and with less formality than in the traditional lending programmes. However, they are not small industries specific except in rare cases. They usually serve to anyone in their locality who can save and borrow effectively.

6.3.2 Production

A number of problems that reduce production efficiency of small business in DCs are linked to the following factors:

- Limited availability of technology.
- Low level of available technology.
- Inadequate fabrication facilities.
- Inappropriate working environment.
- Inappropriate factory layout leading to poor process flows.
- Inadequate local capability to maintain machinery and equipment.
- Inadequate supply of spare parts.
- Poor quality of raw materials.

One of the most obvious problems that reduce production efficiency of small firms in DCs is their utilization of traditional technology.

In many DCs, there is limited availability of technology. Most technology available is imported. Efforts to reduce this importation of technology have led to the pressure of local sourcing in many DCs. Attempts have therefore been made to produce the required technology internally.

While these efforts of local content of technology through inward sourcing are recommendable in view of the long run effects, it has been discovered that many small businesses in the DCs are suffering from short-comings because, where the fabricating industries succeed in producing machinery and equipment, these machines lack functioning ability. Lack of necessary fabrication facilities is one of the major reasons behind the low performance of this machinery and equipment.

Imported machines also suffer from low efficiency because of a lack of indigenous expertise for their installation, maintenance and repair.

Many imported machines are used ones and mostly not modern.

Some are even imported in non-working condition with the hope of repair at home. Anything is acceptable, especially in the small scale sector, as they cannot afford quality equipment because of their poor bargaining power.

Lack of foreign exchange and import restrictions have further reduced the general possibility of importation and hence the volume of technology available. This problem is not limited to small business alone, but hits them harder than their large counterparts.

In many cases machinery and equipment is idle as there is nobody to repair it. In cases where repairs are done, it is a matter of trial and error and the machines are often breaking down due to improper repairs. Added to this is shortage of spare parts of maintaining or repairing available foreign or local machinery.

The services of qualified foreign or local manpower are usually too costly for the small business to afford especially on a regular base. In addition, many small businesses employ untrained workers and operate in congested or unsuitable buildings. They also have no testing facilities and quality control is minimal, consequently, a large proportion of their products come out very poor in quality and standard.

There is evidence that productivity is relatively low in many small firms because they still employ traditional method of production which have failed to keep up with the speed of new techniques or modern technology.

Factory layout is poor in many small business operations, and only simple or outdated machinery is used. In Indonesia for example, a small scale industry roof tile manufacture in Madura has a relatively high rejected rate. In these instances, the problems were due to low quality of raw materials and workers as well as inadequate organisation of work procedures. A study of small business in metal working industries in Malaysia and Indonesia found that continuous use of obsolete and less efficient machinery and equipment was the most important production related problem of SSIs. All these problems contribute significantly to production inefficiency in many small businesses in DCs.

6.3.3 Personnel

Generally small businesses in DCs are run by entrepreneurs who have little or no education or training. They are also staffed with workers who suffer from the same deficiency. Most small scale owners/ manager and employees acquire their training through apprenticeship training which is the most formalized training scheme operated in most DCs. This scheme provides over 50% of employment in small business sector, including the men and women who act as proprietors of small business.

A number of factors have been identified to combine to reduce effectiveness of this apprenticeship system.

Training is usually carried out by the small business entrepreneurs or senior employees. It is a known fact that a man can only teach what he knows and his effectiveness as a teacher in part depends on the teaching facilities at his disposal.

Many small business entrepreneurs have little or no formal education.

The knowledge which they pass on to their trainees had been acquired through a similar apprenticeship. Also the facilities available to them are in many cases rudimentary and inadequate. The problem is worsened by the low quality of the trainees themselves. Many of them have no formal education while the great majority of those who have formal education do not have more than elementary education. Such a low educational background makes the task of training more difficult. Besides, many trainees have only drifted to the apprenticeship training system for lack of alternative employment opportunities rather than out of genuine interest to acquire the skills being taught. In consequence, the motivation to learn is low and it is not unusual to see some trainees abandoning their training before the scheduled time. In consequence, many of the products of the system are at best inadequate.

Added to this is the fact that small businesses generally do not have the resources to conduct any formal training programmes or send their workers for out of plant training. Most seriously, small businesses have problems recruiting workers or even keep the good ones.

It could be argued that a good competent group of employees is an essential fact for the success of any business. Finding and keeping good employees is not a matter of luck but rather the result of aggressive recruitment, careful selection, proper training and motivation including thoughtful management. Often because of lack of fund, small businesses are not able to afford the employment and retaining of qualified staff to man their production processes and output.

The competitive advantage of small business as explained earlier may well be the close personal relationship or contact. Often, the performance standards or success of small business is however complicated by close personal relation since it often happens that job and competence are usually considered on private or personal relationship. The business is usually managed along personal or family line, without much consideration of competence and performance.

Among many reasons for problems encountered in this area is the use of family labour especially in strategic positions. Usually family members occupy strategic positions in many small businesses, in order to maintain the needed owner/manager influence or authority. In most cases employment is not based on competence but personal relationship.

This usually affects the overall performance of the small scale industry in question. Workers are generally reluctant to work in small business sector which offer worse pay and inferior terms of working conditions compared to the large ones. For the same reasons, many workers tend to leave the small business as soon as they have acquired a certain level of skill or experience. This problem has grown more acute in countries where there is shortage of skilled manpower.

In Malaysia for example, the difficulty in attracting and retaining skilled workers especially in metal tradesmen is considered the most pressing problem faced by the small scale metal working industries. Small scale metal industries cannot pay attractive wages, and their working environment is extremely poor, largely a result of inadequate factory facilities. There are also some countries where small firms have been relying on the use of part-time workers. The use of part-time workers is not without problem because there is the tendency for these workers to leave their jobs during certain seasons such as the growing or harvesting season. This is the case in Malaysia.

6.3.4 Marketing

Marketing problems faced by small firms in DCs could be grouped into:

- Problems associated with the products.
- Poor packaging and design.
- Inadequacy of product quality and standard.
- Problems associated with market environment.

The marketing activities of small firms in DCs are not always visible or obvious to an outsider observer. Perception of what the term marketing meant to small business owner did not always match what some owners did in practice.

Many small businesses in DCs have unprompted definition of marketing. They usually focus mainly on customer acquisition and promotion while identifying customer needs.

The small business inadequate resources for indentifying market outlets, market characteristics of the products, and also tapping the existing or known market outlets and contacts combine to make up market and environmental associated problems. These inadequate resources and environmental problems are traced to:

- Poor raw material inputs.
- Poor transport systems.
- Competition.

A number of small businesses have problems with marketing their products because of a number of factors like:

- ✓ Poor designs, which are both inefficient and inartistic.
- ✓ Low quality of finished products due to the use of poor quality raw materials.
- ✓ Inadequate machines imported second hand or fabricated locally.

- ✓ Insufficient quality control.
- ✓ Lack of precision due to inadequate equipment and lack of skilled personal.
- ✓ Lack of after sales services.

As long as the small firm sells its products through middlemen, some of the problems related to marketing like advertising and product design, may be avoided and not without related problems. Many small firms tend to leave marketing to middlemen, so they know almost nothing about changes in demand for their products, price fluctuations, changes in consumer taste or other market trends. Some enterprises even borrow their materials from the same middlemen to whom they entrust their marketing and are subsequently not free to sell to other middlemen.

On the other hand, small firms that sell their products directly experience difficulties in various areas of marketing as many lacks or have problems in acquiring the skills to market their products effectively.

Many small businesses in DCs also have problems in acquiring marketing information. The few institutional sources of information, where necessary marketing data may be obtained are too expensive for small enterprises and generally, the information available are not specific or tailored to small business needs. Any sale information is therefore obtained usually by chance, and only fragmentarily derived from suppliers, customers, other manufacturers and from personal observations. Altogether, the information available does not form a sufficient basis, even to plan medium-term investment and production levels.

Small businesses in DCs also have great problems in selling to the government or the export market. The government imposes certain requirements which small businesses are unable to meet, such as the size of the order or the delivery schedule. There are also costs involved in making contact with the government department awaiting business relations. Similarly, exporting involves substantial expenses in terms of participation in trade fairs and missions abroad. Even if they can afford these expenses, the relatively high production cost and low quality of their products make it difficult for SSIs to compete.

The products of many small firms in DCs are not standardized and are relatively small in quantity. Their products are therefore restricted to the local market.

Although the small business products can be some of the inputs of large scale enterprises, the non standardization of their products restricts their access to national and international markets, so. Non-harmonization of the production process of small business continues to restrict their marketing horizons-limited possibilities of market expansion and the absence of a steady, guaranteed market.

Difficulties in transportation appear as another importance factor, influencing the severity of raw materials supply and procurement.

An industrial research (Barry 2010) done in Haiti for example, revealed that most small enterprises that experience larger than average raw material problems are those which are least accessibly by road, and as such, raw material problems are strongly related to transportation. This problem is not limited to Haiti alone, but is almost general in many DCs due to the low level of their transportation system.

Another market barrier sometimes overlooked in the concept stage of a small business is the need to have access to established channels of distribution. A small business marketing a new product may face an uphill struggle to win space on the shelves of the major retailers.

The non promotional aspects of marketing such as product development, pricing and distribution were highly ignored by many small businesses in DCs.

There are small businesses in DCs who have been found to have completely ignored or are reluctant to respect marketing as a business function. Some of the reasons associated with this negative behaviour to marketing activities by small business owner managers include:

- ✓ Marketing is regarded as something for a larger company and of little practical use to the small business.
- ✓ Marketing has a long term contribution to a business - when small business owners tend to think short term.

- ✓ Marketing has no direct qualitative effect upon the business - when small business owners are thought to be pragmatic, cash in hand, sales minded people.
- ✓ Marketing combats the small business from its entrepreneurial culture.
- ✓ Marketing is an expensive function to run – for the small business, good marketing personnel are hard to find and demand higher salaries that they deserve.
- ✓ Advert and selling provide a better return on investment - than the more all embracing activity known as marketing.
- ✓ Small business entrepreneurs show themselves to be the personification of the marketing concept.
- ✓ The proximity of owner/manager to the market place helps appreciate the needs of the customer and therefore respond to changes in the market demand.

6.3.5 The Small Business Owner/Manager

Some of the management problems of the small business can be traced to the business owner/managers in DCs who share a number of characteristics that have become a source or management problems.

Many small business owner/managers in DCs lack managerial training as most of them started their business based on their technical experience or apprenticeship, with no formal education and management knowledge of how to run a successful business.

Small firms in DCs are found to lack financial resources and time required to carry out successful business management.

Where some applications of principles of management actually take place in a small firm, it tends to be by chance and different from that carried out traditionally. Most small firms in DCs do not see formal management principles as a necessity, and small business owner/managers in DCs are accused of applying business management principles based on principles in their heads, only to execute it at will as the owner/manager feels.

Critics of the need for systematic application of management principles in small business argued that management (especially strategic planning) loses its meaning in a dynamic environment where innovation, flexibility and responsiveness to perishable opportunities are key conditions for survival, and the knowledge and the process of environmental forecasting becomes almost meaningless and long range planning of questionable value. Management is considered contingent upon the nature of the business, the skills of the owner manager and his/her predisposition to management, business size, and stage of development/life cycle stage. In practice, small business planning tends to simply keep doing what they have done before, assuming that market conditions will continue as before and hope for the best. The application of management principles in small business is more or less limited.

Despite all these criticisms, it is important to point out that the small business owner/manager will in no doubt, need management for the successful start-up and running of the business activities. Management is the process by which the small business owner/manager should use to develop the firm's business goals/objectives, mission/purpose, strategies, and maintain the firm's competitiveness in the market place.

It is important to recognise that small business owner/managers should involve themselves in the learning and understanding of management principles. One important reason is that it is usually the owner-manager of small business who is seen as the ultimate strategist and decision maker in the firm. Studies within application of management in small business expound the benefits and stress the associated improved organisational performance. For small businesses operating within the turbulent developing environment of DCs, where conditions are subject to constant changes, the knowledge and application of management becomes inevitable

Further reading

Akrasanel N et al, (1983), Rural of Farm Employment in Thailand, BangkoK.

Arief, K. (1992), Small Scale Industries and Small Enterprise Credit Programmes in Indonesia.

Baumback, C. (1983), Basic Small Business Management, Prentice Hall, Eaglewood Cliff, New York.

Bautista, R. (1988), Macro Policies and Technology Choice in the Philippines.

Berry, A. (1988), The Relevance of Small Scale Industries New York.

Bolnik, B. (1982), Commercial Credit for Small Business: Bulleting of Indonesia Economic Studies.

Byke and Sengenberger Brusco, S. (1993), Small Firms and the Provision of Real Services.

Cheng Peng Lim (1990), Development of Small Business in Developing Countries, NY.

PART 4

TECHNICAL ASSISTANCE AND SMALL BUSINESS IN DEVELOPING COUNTRIES (DCS)

INTRODUCTION

The preceding part and chapters have identified management problems of small business in DCs,

This part will include chapters 7 and 8 of this book. Chapter 7 will give us an introductory insight into the nature and background of technical assistance that will cover necessary areas technical assistance concerned with developing small business in DCs. Chapter 8 will introduce UNIDO technical assistance and relevance as well as impact on small business in DCs.

CHAPTER 7

TECHNICAL ASSISTANCE AND SMALL BUSINESS IN DCS

Aim

To introduce the nature and need for technical assistance to small business in DCs.

Objectives

After studying this chapter you should be able to:

- Understand the meaning technical assistance.
- Explain relationship between technical and aid.
- Describe forms of technical assistance.

7.1 Introduction

The need for technical assistance for small businesses found in the DCs could be drawn down to the various management problems and related factors reviewed in chapter 6.

For adequate promotional measures and for a positive result, these problems need urgent attention and, if possible, solutions, so that the potential advantages of small business, as analysed in chapter 2, can be fully realized.

DCs aware of at least some of these problems have indeed been trying to put up measures to solve them. While these efforts are commendable, many DCs are handicapped in achieving maximum satisfaction due to limited resources. These resources are either not available or are being under-utilised or not even exploited. Assistance is therefore needed externally to help in either improving the available resources or supplementing them.

A lot of external assistance in various forms and categories has therefore been sought by many DCs for this purpose.

The United Nations, through its funding and executing agencies, have been very active in giving various forms of assistance to DCs, aimed at reducing their predicaments.

7.2 Technical Assistance - Definitions

Currently, the terms "technical assistance" and "technical co-operation" are used interchangeably to mean the same.

Technical cal assistance (sometimes compared to technical co-operation), has been defined by a number of individuals and organisations from their various perspectives.

The Organisation for Economic Co-operation and Development (OECD), for statistical collection purpose defines technical co-operations as "Activities where the primary purpose is to augment the level of knowledge, skill, technical know-how or production aptitude of DCs i.e. increasing the stock of human intellectual capital or their capacity for more effective use of their existing factor endowment", while technical assistance is defined as "financing service with the primary purpose of contributing to the design and/ or implementation of a project or programme aiming to increase the physical capital stock of the recipient country."

The DAC provides the following definition. "Technical co-operation encompasses the whole range of assistance activities designed to improve the level of skills, knowledge, technical knowhow and productive aptitudes of the DCs" A particularly important objectives of the technical assistance is institutional development i.e., the contribution to the strengthening and improved functioning of the many institutions essential for sustainable development through effective management and operation of an economy and society more generally.

The World Bank reports on technical assistance and related documents and studies use various definitions. The following is the most recent ones, set down in a review of the Bank's technical assistance programmes defining technical as "transfer or adaptation of ideas, knowledge, practices, technologies, or skills to foster economic development". The purposes of World Bank technical assistance are classified as follows:

- ✓ Policy development.
- ✓ Institutional development.

- ✓ Capacity building.
- ✓ Project and programme support.

The UNDP has the following definitions in its guidelines for statistical collection in the Development Co-operation Information Centre: "Technical co-operation comprises the provision of resources aimed at transfer of skills and knowhow and capacity building within national institutions to undertake development activities". It includes resources in form of personnel (international, national, long, short-term).

Further, technical co-operation may broadly be divided into two categories:

(a) Investment-related or technical co-operation input necessary to assist the implementation of capital investment projects.
(b) General institutional support for free study of investment projects provided regardless of need for specific investment projects.

Also, there are definitions that set out the purpose of technical co-operation to guide UNDP in its operational purposes. This definition was developed in 1975 as part of a major review of the purpose of technical co-operation in the United Nations (UN) system, because of a need to set policies for the requirement of DCs. The basic purpose of technical assistance co-operation should be the promotion of self reliance in DCs, by building up inter-alia, production capacity and their indigenous resources, by increasing the availability of managerial and technical administration and research capacities required in the development process.

From these definitions, it could be pointed out that a common feature that exists among them is that technical assistance has a common objective. It consists of transfer or transmission of essential economic resources, like knowledge or technique, materials or human resources, and it is aimed at helping those who receive it to solve specific problems in a more suitable manner, in keeping up with their needs.

Improvements in the economic situation of all nations, especially through policy, institutional and enterprise-development aimed at self reliance, are the central objectives of technical assistance.

Nothing counts more for the development of nations than efficient resource management. How efficient resource management is applied varies among countries and over time.

From the perspective of global improvement of the economy of all nations, efficiency in the management of national resources does not mean only the pursuit of increased output in a given economy, but also requires the complex consideration and assistance to poorer nations who also need economic growth, without which, poverty would continue in this area and their resources would continue to be wasted.

Many years ago, when technical assistance came into being, there were high hopes that along with capital assistance will bring fundamental changes, speeding up economic growth and reducing poverty especially among poorer nations. Technical assistance was at that time considered a simple concept. Today, the concept is recognized as being more than a simple concept.

Although the essentials of technical assistance might be easily grasped, numerous complexities surround the concept and confusion has grown up around its use, especially in the use of key concept: technical assistance and technical co-operation.

As explained earlier, the terms "technical assistance" and "technical co-operation" are used interchangeably to mean the same. This is also the case in this book. The word "technical assistance" is generally used here to cover both concepts - technical assistance and technical co-operation.

7.3 Technical Assistance and Aid

As much as it is relevant to understand both terms - technical assistance and technical co-operation, it is also useful to understand the relationship between technical assistance and aid.

In the case of the DCs, aid is transferred in many ways. The more important forms include:

- Project aid.
- Programme aid.
- Bilateral and multilateral aid.
- Technical assistance.
- Food aid.
- Emergency aid.

Project and programme aids are competing categories: if aid is not for a project then necessarily it is for a programme - the latter being a flexibly interpreted term for all non-project aid - bilateral and multilateral aid.

Food aid, technical assistance etc, support either a project or programme.

Generally, these forms of aid are not mutually exclusive but interrelated or could be used in combination; project aid could consist of bilateral food aid or bilateral technical assistance. There can be multilateral food aid and multilateral technical assistance or emergency assistance.

However, these forms of aids and technical assistance need to be distinguished, since each category possesses certain individual characteristics.

7.4 Forms of Technical Assistance

Technical assistance as a kind of aid assumes a very wide variety of forms. These include:

- Visits of experts and technicians.
- Receiving fellowship training.
- Organizing courses and seminars.
- Exchanging and disseminating information or documents.
- Supplying material and equipment and occasionally finance, etc.

Technical assistance is probably the oldest form of external aid. It is also one of the most significant and critical forms of development co-operation.

Technical assistance can also be of many levels:

- Macro policy support.
- Institutional building.
- Direct support to enterprises.
- Direct human training.

In the early stages of technical assistance, most efforts were mainly on macro policy support, concentrated on areas such as direct human training, especially after the colonial period; to help bridge the colonial gap. Official technical assistance in DCs has its roots in the colonial rule and the subsequent decolonization process. The colonial situation somehow inhibited the development of technical skills and the emergence of competence in management in DCs. There was a common assumption that as the bulk of the educated indigenous lobour force in DCs expanded, the need for technical assistance would decline.

The issue of institution building is currently taking much more attention. As stated in many of the definition introduced above, one of the essential aspects of technical assistance is institution building. Recent international debates on technical assistance have focused attention on the importance of institutional development or capacity building in strengthening the indigenous capacity of many DCs to help them manage economic change and growth in their various countries.

There is growing consensus that the development of these capacities should be the central point, if not the unique goal, of technical assistance.

In its principles for new guideline in technical assistance, DAC states: "progress towards sustained, more equitable and self reliant development depends critically on the strength and quality of a country's institutional capacity. Contributing to this objective must therefore be an essential purpose of development co-operation in general and technical assistance in particular, as aid actively cannot be regarded as successful unless it has contributed to strengthening the local institution through which and for which it works".

In many DCs, the policy statement on technical assistance emphasise the capacity building aspect of technical assistance. For example, the government of Malawi's policy document in 1990, entitled "Statement of Policy on Technical Assistance for Human and Institutional Development", considers its technical assistance programmes carried out in close collaboration with donor communities as a major means for building up the country's institution and human capabilities to execute national development programmes. This is just one example from many reasons for the renewed emphasis on institutional development in capacity building. Perhaps, the clearest lesson of the many years of development efforts are that weak performance of indigenous institution is one of the biggest bottlenecks to foster. After receiving aid local institution have to be able to continue technical assistance after the external technical assistance is stopped.

Further reading

DAC (1991), Development Assistance Committee: Principles for New Orientation in Technical Cooperation.
ILO (2000), Group Based Savings and Credits for Local Poor, ILO, Geneva.
ILO (1986), The Promotion of Small Scale Industries Vol.1.
ILO (2000), Towards Full Employment Production for Columba, ILO
OECD (1988), The Newly Industrialising Countries, Challenges and Opportunity for OECD Countries, Paris.
OECD (1985), Creating Jobs at the Local Level, Paris.
UNDP (2000), Human Development Report, New York.
UNDP, NaTCAP (2001), Methodology Regional Bureau report for Africa.
UNDP (1990), Project In-depth Evaluation- A Briefing Kit, Central Evaluation Office, New York.
UNDP Annual Reports, Vienna 1989 – 2000.
UNIDO (1991 -2000), Country Brief on Agro-related Metal working Industries in LDC in the Asia and Pacific regions.
UNIDO (1990), Development of the African Traditional Textile Industry Vienna, Austria.
UNIDO (1989), Human Resources in Sri Lanka's Industrial
UNIDO (2000), Information Report Paper, Vienna, Austria.
UNIDO (1999), Nigeria Experience on Industrial Project Evaluation, Lagos, Nigeria.
UNIDO: Nigerian Industrial Research Review Series, 1999 -2001.
UNIDO (1991), Stimulating Rural Small Industries in Developing
UNIDO (1993), The Present Situation of Small and Medium Enterprises in Kenya and Tanzania and impact of Structural Adjustment policy
Weiss, J. (1988), Industry in Developing Countries: Theory, Policy and Evidence, London.
World Assembly of Small Scale Industries, Rabat Symposium on IDDA 1986.
Young, A. (1988), Small Scale Business development, New York.

CHAPTER 8

THE UNIDO/UNDP TECHNICAL ASSISTANCE FOR SMALL BUSINES IN DCS

Aim

To introduce UNIDO/UNDP technical assistance in DCs.

Objectives

After studying this chapter you should be able to:

- Describe the development of UNIDO/UNDP technical assistance in DCs.
- Explain the significance of UNIDO response to small business needs in DCs.
- Describe UNIDO Technical Assistance in Nigeria.
- Outline errors and problems associated with technical assistance projects in DCs.

8.1 The UNIDO/UNDP Technical Assistance

For the United Nation Industrial Development Organisation (UNIDO), and United Nation Industrial Development Programme (UNDP), technical assistance is one of the earliest manifestations of the will of the international community, to honour the pledge in the United Nations Character of 1948, to promote the economic and social advancement of all people.

In that year, at the Third Session, the General Assembly unanimously adopted a resolution (200/111) creating the United Nations Technical Assistance Programme. This modest start was followed by the creation of the expanded programme of technical assistance.

The programme's purpose was to help the DCs to strengthen their national economies, through the development of their industries and agriculture, with a view to promoting their economic and political independence in the spirit of the charter, and to ensure the attainment of higher levels of economic and social welfare for the entire population.

In 1966, the expanded programme of technical assistance was merged into the single United Nation Development Programme-UNDP.

Under the United Nations (UN) system, the United Nation Development Programme (UNDP) is one of the principal funding organs.

The UNDP currently carries out its technical projects through the so called "executive agencies". The United Nations Industrial Development Organisation (UNIDO) is one of its principle executive agencies in the area of small business or small scale industries.

UNIDO is the 16th special agency of the United Nations system since Jan 1. 1986.

Prior to its status, UNIDO existed as an autonomous organ within the United Nations secretariat in 1966.

A significant organisation transformation goes back to the 1975 Second General Conference which adopted the Lima Declaration and Plan of Action calling for the strengthening of UNIDO in order to increase its ability to render assistance to the DCs in the most efficient way.

In 1979, a plenipotentiary conference adopted a constitution stipulating that UNIDO's primary objective would be the promotion of industrial development in the DCs. Along this line, a number of supports and special programme activities have therefore been mapped out to enable UNIDO achieve these objectives.

Main support activities of UNDIO include:

- Global, regional, national and sectoral studies.
- Statistical studies and surveys.
- Studies of technical activities, technology acquisition, and technology development and application.
- Industrial and technological information bank INTIB.
- Investment promotion services, experts meeting and an industrial forum.
- Solidarity meetings for co-operation between DCs.

Main special programmes include:

- Consultations, providing an opportunity for all interested in a particular industry, from government, private sector and labour to come together to talk about problems and evaluate them.
- Long term investment promotion.
- Programme and project developments.
- Technology transfer.
- Industrial co-operation among DCs.
- Industrial Development Decade for Africa (IDDA).
- Assistance to least developed countries.
- Co-operation with industrial enterprises and non government organisation.
- Integration of women in the industrial development.

The activities within technical assistance co-operation cover various industrial areas like:

- Agro based industry.

- Engineering industry.
- Chemical industry.
- Metallurgical industry.
- Industrial planning, institutional infrastructure, industrial management and rehabilitation, feasibility studies, industrial human resources management, industrial project, industrial technology transfer, etc.

Usually UNIDO technical assistance to small business is intended to be complementary to host country activities. The normal procedure is making technical assistance available at the explicit request of the host country.

The extent, to which technical assistance in support of small business will be provided in most cases, depends on the priority it is accorded in the host countries national development programme and the available resource for the purpose.

The nature and the role of technical assistance usually vary from one country to another, in most cases depending on the level of economic development.

As already mentioned, the nature of technical assistance can take the form either project or programme. Technical assistance projects for small industries could either be at stimulating new small business development, or in improving or supporting the existing ones. Approaches towards these differ from countries and from agencies as regards the different needs, on various levels of technical assistance applications. According to some literature reviews, the policy level has not been so popular among recipient countries. Usually this type of assistance has been considered as an interference with their internal affairs.

To deal directly with the target group, direct support to entrepreneurs is also given. However, donors and agencies have a marked preference for technical assistance for institutional building. This is based on the expectation that such an institution in due course, can take over the activities previously carried out with external assistance, and that the demand for these activities will be sustained after external technical assistance has come to an end.

As in the areas of work of UNIDO, the promotion of small businesses is carried out mainly through technical co-operation projects and through research and meetings, which are undertaken as supporting activities, aimed principally at facilitating the establishment of national machinery for the development of industries especially, in the small scale sector.

Projects of relatively long duration (two-five years) and involving an important contribution from the United Nation, and from respective government, are in form of experts, fellowship training and equipment, and are undertaken under the special fund component of UNDP.

Shorter operation of more scope is carried out under the technical assistance for special industrial services.

Institutional aspects, which are the focus of technical assistance projects and programmes provided by UNIDO, usually concentrate on building or establishing small business serving institutions. The institutional service may range from policy support institutions (e.g. policy forming bodies found in many DCs), general purpose institutions (e.g., Small and Medium Scale industries Association), functionally based institutions (e.g. Production Centre's, Co-operative institutes, financial Institutions), Vocational Centers, Nongovernmental Organisation, trade associations, etc.

In the DCs, technical assistance provided by UNIDO for institution building may include assistance in establishing and stretching appropriate institutions to serve the small businesses. This has usually been through:

- Establishment and transfer of facilities connected with the small business serving institutions.
- Assisting in choice and use of appropriate technology.
- Designing and carrying out training programmes to develop national capabilities required for the institution of small business.
- Conducting workshop and seminars or related matters.

Since 1986, UNIDO has been active in delivering technical assistance to various DCs in their bid for economic development especially in the area of small business development through institution building.

In African regions, this is carried out within the overall framework of the United Nations Programme for African Economic Recovery and Development (UNPAERD) and the objective of Industrial Development Decade for Africa (IDDA), which has witnessed a number of Structural Adjustment Programmes in many African countries.

In the Lagos Plan of Action for IDDA, the development of small business was viewed as one of the main strategy for creating self reliance and self-sustaining sound industrial base for the African countries with emphasis on the development of capacities and capabilities.

The need for the establishment of national and sub regional industrial policies was therefore stressed, aimed at establishing small businesses which could contribute to the much needed industrial base and promoting resource base industries such as Agro-based, basic engineering, chemical, metallurgical, etc.

Also it was emphasised that the contribution of small businesses to the implementation of IDDA programme would be greatly enhanced once the scope of their activities has been determined, appropriate capacities developed, and basic infrastructures made available.

In line with these, the following activities – in areas of policy formulation and implementation, institutional framework including essential project activities were considered at national, regional and sub regional levels.

- At national level:

    - ✓ Formulating policies, strategies, and a coherent and integrated development programme for development of small business with the framework of industrial development, and taking into account possibilities for inter-sectoral and interlinked project activities.

- ✓ Assessing manpower and managerial capabilities, and establishing a programme for their upgrading, involving country-wide identification and registration of entrepreneurs (including potential entrepreneurs, and the organisation of national small business and rural industrial associations).
- ✓ Facilitating the marketing of final products, procurement of raw materials and intermediate inputs etc, at stable prices, though specially designed national marketing corporations for small business.
- ✓ Designing training programmes for upgrading extension services and developing national capacities in projects identifications: promotion, design, analysis and implementations for development of small business.
- ✓ Undertaking action-oriented research on the possibility of establishing for the procurement of equipment for small business and rural industries, and establishing effective linkages with the development of local engineering design and production capacities, including standardization and quality control as well as advisory and institutional support.
- ✓ Formulating arrangement for subcontracting between SSI and large scale industries.
- ✓ Studying the most efficient means of providing physical facilities for small business project, including water, electricity, and building especially in rural areas and investigating possibilities for rural co-operatives through the provision of infrastructure, such as industrial estate and workshops.
- ✓ Re-orienting and mobilizing decentralised industrial service and institutions to serve, for agriculture, consumer goods in the basic needs category, and linkages with urban industry and markets.

- At sub regional and regional levels:

    ✓ Preparing a directory of project profiles for the whole of Africa, covering techno-economic information and including products to be manufactured, process descriptions, capacity and specification of plant and machinery, raw materials and other inputs, financial requirements, in the form of fixed and working capital, marketing and products distribution, and a programme of action to assist and advice SSIs entrepreneurs in the manufacturing activities.
    ✓ Encouraging new forms of multinational co-operation through national focal points, responsible for small business and integrated rural development, aimed at broadening the scope, nature there, feasibility, implementation and development of SSI and rural industrial programmes and projects.
    ✓ Formulating and implementing technical co-operation programmes among the African countries, as with other developing countries, to include study tours, in-plant training, workshop, seminars and training courses involving officials, trainees, experts and small business entrepreneurs.
    ✓ Providing appropriate support to institutions to promote self-help in small business undertakings, including special funds and agencies to provide financial assistance in form of risk capital; customs and tax exemptions; loans and specific projects; technical repair and maintenance brigades to provide service at a fee, consultancy service, internal and external market promotion, marketing and procurement, and training of workers, managers, foremen and entrepreneurs.
    ✓ Establishment of national institutions to design training programme for upgrading extension services, provide

- ✓ information, consultation and extension services, and foster capabilities in development of small business and rural industries.
- ✓ Establishment of appropriate support institution and mechanism to promote self-help in small business activities, mobilise funds for the development of these industries, procure raw materials, intermediate inputs etc. and market products.
- ✓ Creation of multinational associations of small business through national focal points.

In line with this framework, UNIDO assistance was requested by some of the governments in DCs to help in carrying out comprehensive services to foster their industrial reconstruction and development plans.

For example, in the oil producing DCs, the weak situation in the oil market has led to a continued effort to reduce their dependence on oil in their industrial and economic structure. Stress has been put on the private sector and small business development in their industrialisation effort, and impetus given by the governments through the creation of supporting institutions.

In conclusion, it is necessary to point out that the importance of technical assistance varies from country to country. Whatever is the importance, it has unfortunately been a neglected resource. In relation to its financial and developmental significance, technical assistance seems to have been undermanaged and under-utilised. Details of errors encountered in technical assistance projects (UNIDO in particular) are treated later in this chapter.

8.2 UNIDO Response to Small Business Management Problems in Developing Countries (DCs)

As explained earlier, UNIDO is one of the executive agencies of the UNDP. For UNIDO, there is evidence that small business management handicaps in DCs have been fully recognized. UNIDO has therefore provided technical assistance to help the DCs raise their share in the world industrial output.

For example, in October 1986, the industrial development board decided to include the first consultation on small and medium scale industries including co-operatives in the programme of system of consultations.

In order to assist small businesses effectively in various DCs, UNIDO carried out studies analyzing the problems and constraints to small firms in the DCs. Some of the major analysed areas include:

- Environment favorable to sustain the growth of small business.
- Productivity improvement.
- Financing of small business.
- International and regional co-operation.

In line with these, UNIDO has been involved in technical assistance at various levels.

In the area of institutional building, which is the main concentration of this thesis, UNIDO has been involved in various projects and programmes of assistance to institutions serving small business.

Projects and programme of assistance provided by UNIDO in these respect have been either in upgrading existing institutions or starting new ones.

The general aims for providing technical assistance for developing small business service institutions have been discussed earlier. This is also true in the case of UNIDO technical assistance for small business service institutions, aiming at helping them stand on their own, so they would be able to continue the technical assistance in absence of UNIDO.

Areas of UNIDO institutional assistance always try to cover problem areas of the small business. Technical assistance to institutions serving the small business mostly addressed the major problems confronting the small business such as:

- ✓ Lack of technical skill.
- ✓ Difficult access to credit.
- ✓ Lack of marketing skill.
- ✓ Problems in organisation.
- ✓ Technical problems.
- ✓ Installation and equipment.
- ✓ Lack of accounting skill.
- ✓ Access to raw material and information systems, etc.

The responding technical assistance interventions to these problems cover areas like training, extension services, research, technology transfer, fellowship, including consultations etc., to help in institutional building and possible sustenance, which would further aid the small business development. For example, the policy support institutions like the policy analyses department in Nigeria, multipurpose institutions e.g., SIDO Tanzania, Nigeria, Zambia, Kenya and Egypt. Haiti Agricultural Development Institute, Pakistan Leader Production and Development Centre, Central Metallurgical Centre's in Nigeria, Egypt, Kenya, Zambia and Tanzania including many Development Banks and other organisations like the Non Governmental Organisations, Small Business Trade Associations, have all received technical assistance in various forms from UNIDO, to establish or improve their services to small business.

Areas like the supply of information at the country level in particular for the priority sectors like the small business is crucial for the success of the industrial development in the DCs. However, the position in this regard at present needs considerable improvement. Several DCs do not have an industrial information system themselves and in many cases where they have such facilities, they are mostly in the nature of documentation services. They also suffer a lack of adequate resources to systematically obtain data from external sources.

According to the United Nations (UN) General Assembly Resolution 3507, the Industrial and Technological Information Bank (INTIB) was set up in 1980 to facilitate and accelerate the industrial and technological information flow to the DCs for the selection of alternative technologies and equipment and reduce the preparation time of feasibility studies. INTIB has therefore been helping in the creation of national industrial and technological information systems and networks in the DCs.

For example, in Nigeria, Zambia, Tanzania, Kenya etc. which have been selected as part of the Industrial Development Decade for Africa (IDDA) programme, technical assistance have been provided to strengthen their national information systems.

The metallurgical industries section of the UNIDO, has since its introduction been assisting the DCs with expansion, modernization, and introduction of quality control in the existing plants. The development of metallurgical research centers has also occupied an important place as the small business cannot show any appreciable progress unless supported and backed by compatible research facilities.

UNIDOs metallurgical industries section has accordingly assisted various DCs either in the establishment of new metallurgical centers, as in Egypt, Nigeria, Pakistan etc. to achieve greater access to finance especially credit, technology, including improvement in general management skills, seen by UNIDO as major determinants of economics success.

In the area of finance, marketing, accounting skills, many small businesses in DCs have received UNIDO equipment, organisation technical skills etc. A number of commercial and development banks have received technical assistance in form of training and equipment transfer, for improvements in staff skills and institutional capabilities for services to small business. For example, National Food Industry Research in Vietnam, Hydrated Leader Footwear Centre in Pakistan, Federal Institute for Industrial Research Oshodi- Nigeria, is just few examples to mention.

There are some indications that quiet a number of the technical assistance projects have been relevant, efficient, effective and sustaining, with clear impact on small businesses. Unfortunately there are cases of failure, due to errors made and associated problems encountered before and during the course of projects management.

In Vietnam, as a positive example, completion of the strengthening of the National Food Industry Research Institute contributed to upgrading the local and professional skills with special regard to applied food technology. Also the Hydrated Leather Footwear Centre in Pakistan had positive impact. Trainees from the local small business completed curses in footwear design and pattern making, a substantial increase in productivity was achieved in the only mechanized factory and the facilities in the centre were increasingly used by small business. Equipment for a latex pilot plant was installed in a development centre for Rubber Technology in Myanmar. Training courses on quality control and mould design were attended by thirty six participants from the central and local manufacturing units. Four rubber plants at Yangon and Myanmar benefited from direct assistance in testing basic and auxiliary new moulds. Links were established with similar institution in Malaysia and Sri Lanka. There is another interesting impact from some projects studied, concerning the role of women in economic development. This is considered as being very important, regarding the potential in women entrepreneur ship which has not been fully realized. Projects undertaken for women involved in garri and salt processing through the Federal Institute of Industrial Research Oshodi are good examples. The impact was felt in the volume of output as in income and social benefits. Although some projects were successful, there are also cases of projects which fail to provide the needed result or impact. Some of the reasons to this are discussed in the next section.

Just like the other DCs reviewed, UNIDO has been active in the transfer of technical assistance for institutions in Nigeria as regards the small business sub- sector.

The background of the interest for technical assistance was the awareness of the federal government of Nigeria that under changing economic conditions due to decreases in world oil prices, and deteriorating situation of the economy, industrialisation and self support becomes vital for the economy of the country, especially regarding small business promotion and development. The government also recognized the need to build an adequate institutional framework at the national and state levels, as an essential prerequisite for rapid and planned economic growth.

Many of the institutions for small business introduced earlier have in the course of the work received technical assistance in one way or the other from UNIDO, to facilitate their preference and activities for small business development in various locations. These institutions include: the Nigerian Bank for Commerce and Industries (NBCI), Nigerian Economic Reconstruction Fund (NERFUND), the Industrial Data Bank (IDB), Federal Institute for Industrial Research Oshogbo (FIIRO), Centre for Industrial Research and Development (CIRD), Industrial Development Centers (IDCs).

Most of these institutions rendering services to small firms have problems with efficiency in their services. Their low efficiency performance is combination of a number of problems they encounter, ranging from lack of fund to inadequate staff and facilities and facilities. They have similar problems with their equipment and computer facilities for feasibility analysis and reporting including skill development of their staff to handle credit and related banking activities, especially to small businesses.

UNIDO has in many ways contributed through its technical assistance activities in the reduction and possible elimination of some of these problems. FIIRO for example has had a number of projects passed through the institution. There has been garri processing project, Salt Water pump project, the water Pump project, and the Information system development projects to mention but a few. In the case of garret and Salt projects, the technology was developed by FIIRO/UNIDO as UNIDO shared the view that FIIRO has a key role to play in adapting technology and research to suit Nigerian conditions.

8.3 Errors and Problems Associated with Technical Assistance Projects in Developing Countries

The aim of this section is not to evaluate all the technical assistance provided by UNIDO in the area of institution building. This is obviously impossible regarding the limited number of projects studied for this work and also, the need for a vast area of information for possible overall evaluation. The aim is rather, to help identify some of the errors that are usually associated with development projects in relation to UNIDO technical assistance projects sofar carried out and reviewed in desk study, as well as personal interview with the respective backstopping officials.

In line with UNDP project evaluation guidelines, evaluation of projects or programme has a number of major points:

- Relevance: did the purpose of the project remain valid and pertinent? Can evidence of the validity and pertinence be provided?
- Effectiveness: did the project achieve its objectives? Were they achievable at all?
- Efficiency: what outputs were produced and how well? Can they be used?
- Sustainability: can the project's results continue to contribute after UNDP assistance has terminated?
- Impact: what effects has the project had on its surroundings?

The UNDP evaluation guideline is primarily a management tool designed to help in decision making, by assessing performance and by providing lessons derived from the experience, providing basis for improvement in development and implementation of future projects or programmes.

For the purpose of this book, the treatment of issues of errors in technical assistance project management has been arranged according to the three major phases in projects cycle:

1. Project design.
2. Project implementation.
3. Project follow -up.

Some errors made and the associated problems encountered during the project design, project implementation and follow up phase, have significant effect on the management of technical assistance projects and therefore, the relevancy, effectiveness, efficiency, sustainable and impact of projects.

Cases of poor project design usually occur as a result of errors made in identification or feasibility studies. Identification refers to the selection of a project theme and target group, while feasibility studies should be used to establish relevant objectives.

Improper identification and poor feasibility studies or lack of them have been found to have led to wrong choice of target groups and project objectives. Some of the reasons behind this include:

- Lack of involvement of the host country.
- Donor sympathy on host country.
- Confusion of terms as regards, objectives, inputs, and activities.

Lack of coherent government policy and involvement in technical assistance projects has led to independent approach by donor agencies in line with their own needs and priorities. This is the case with the Small Industries Development Organisation (SIDO) in Tanzania where as a parastatal; the budget was not integrated in the national planning system. This has led to excessive donor dependency with its effects on the quality of the project design and the choice of target groups. The donor seems to have influenced the type and the kind of assistance provided. Donors themselves have failed to co-ordinate their efforts and benefit from each other's experiences. The institutional strength and ability to sustain does not seem to have been improved.

There are also cases where the host country's agencies, which should have more insight in the policy and institutional environment of the host country, are not fully involved in the identification and feasibility studies before project take off. Identification and feasibility studies made therefore lack the necessary background information needed for proper and reliable identification of target groups and useful objectives. The technical assistance to Senati, in Peru, Women Non-Governmental Organisation in Kenya, Industrial Development Centre at Oshogbo, Nigeria are some example of projects that suffered setbacks as a result of improper or unrealistic identification of host country institutes. In the case of Senati in Peru, this resulted in cash flow problems, and the Industrial Development Centre in Nigeria ended up with wrong staffing of more administrators than trainers.

Mixing up terms like output, activities and objectives has also contributed to poor identification and feasibility studies and poor projects design.

In the implementing stage, some of the problems encountered can be reduced to errors made in project design. Bad design can lead to wrong choice of input for implementation for example, in the use of inappropriate hardware, or foreign staff. Use of sophisticated equipment which often lacks backup, or deployment of expertise which tends to become operational rather than instructive, or wrong choice of expatriates, combine to effect the success in the implementing stage. In many cases, they have been found to have contributed to delays in the take-over of activities by the host country.

Complications also occur when several different agencies are involved in the same projects (host country and foreign experts) which often more than constrain the task of managing the inputs, each with different approaches, for example in budgetary periods and other attitudes especially when it involves projects in various locations. The result may then be absence of focal point. SIDO Tanzania has received assistance from various donors with the complication of co-ordination and harmonization of inputs, each donor trying to create an area of dominance.

Lack of funds has been found as one of the major constraints in project implementation. This has always effected the acquisition of needed projects inputs. The Federal Institute of Industrial Research in Nigeria, Small Industrial Development Organisation in Tanzania,

Zambia and Kenya are some of the institutions that suffered setbacks in the implementation of their projects due to lack of funds. Apart from lack of funds, there are also problems with delays in transfer of funds even when they are available.

Transportation problems are another area noticed as a common problem in project implementation. This is more severe when projects are located in rural areas making regular visits to the project site impossible. Added to this is the lack of infrastructure that characterizes many DCs. This usually reduces the speed of projects commitments. Frequent changes in foreign experts usually affect the implementation process, sometimes requiring a very long period of adjustment. The Financiera Poplar in Columbia suffered from frequent changes of foreign staff while the resident chief technical advisor paid flying visits from time to time.

In the case of follow up of projects, excessive donor agency intervention is one of the major problems. Excessive donor agency intervention in terms of support stimulates dependency and usually puts up a barrier against future host countries taking over projects and hence reduces the chances of sustainability and replicability in general. Excessive support therefore becomes counterproductive in the sense that it diminishes the possibility of projects activities being sustained by it, or by local funding. Sustainability is also related to cost effectiveness. The potential to carry on the technical assistance experience would be greater if it were cost effective. A good project design is very decisive for the positive outcome of the whole project management. No project with bad design has been found to have led to good result. Good identification missions could help avoid most of the problems in the implementation and follow up of a project. An important role in project identification and feasibility studies should be given to host country's agencies that have better insight in the host country policy environment and its institutions.

Further reading

UNDP (2000), Human Development Report, New York.

UNDP, NaTCAP (2001), Methodology Regional Bureau report for Africa.

UNDP (1990), Project In-depth Evaluation- A Briefing Kit, Central Evaluation Office, New York.

UNDP Annual Reports, Vienna 1989 – 2000.

UNIDO (1991 -2000), Country Brief on Agro-related Metal working Industries in LDC in the Asia and Pacific regions.

UNIDO (1990), Development of the African Traditional Textile Industry Vienna, Austria.

UNIDO (1989), Human Resources in Sri Lanka's Industrial.

UNIDO (2000), Information Report Paper, Vienna, Austria.

UNIDO (1999), Nigeria Experience on Industrial Project Evaluation, Lagos, Nigeria.

UNIDO: Nigerian Industrial Research Review Series, 1999 -2001.

UNIDO (1993), The Present Situation of Small and Medium Enterprises in Kenya and Tanzania and impact of Structural Adjustment policy

Weiss, J. (1988), Industry in Developing Countries: Theory, Policy and Evidence, London.

World Assembly of Small Scale Industries, Rabat Symposium on IDDA 1986.

World Bank (1978), Employment and Development of Small Enterprises (sector policy paper), Washington DC.

World Bank (1991), Managing Technical Assistance: reports of the Technical Review Task Force.

Young, A. (1988), Small Scale Business development, New York.

PART 5

IMPROVING SMALL BUSINESS MANAGEMENT AND PERFORMANCE IN DEVELOPING COUNTRIES (DCS)

INTRODUCTION

So far this book began with an introduction to the general characteristics of small business, the particular type of small business found in developing countries (DCs), and the significance and potential roles of small business in DCs. Further, policy objectives/measures, institutional framework and UNIDO technical assistance for small business in DCs are all introduced and fully discussed. Also, the management problems of small business in DCs are specifically identified and analysed, including conclusions and recommendations.

This part will introduce us to ways and activities that need to be introduced and implemented efficiently to improve the management and performance of small business in developing countries.

CHAPTER 9

ACHIEVING SMALL BUSINESS MANAGEMENT AND PERFORMANCE IN DCS

Aim

To identify and recommend ways of improving small business management and performance and promotion in DCs

Objectives

After studying this chapter you should be able to:

- Understand ways of improving external environment for improving small business development and management in DCs.
- Understand ways of improving internal environment for improving small business development and management in DCs.
- Make necessary recommendations.

9.1 Introduction

It has been concluded that DC's have not been able to reap the mounting potential advantages associated with small business development, due to variety of management problems.

There is no doubt that small firms are essential component in the industrial development of most DCs, as significant agents of economic growth and social progress. The realisation of this fact by many governments in DCs has led to a fundamental shift from a long held practice of considering large and integrated plants employing mass production technologies and techniques, as the main road to industrialisation, to promoting small business in DCs. However, the possibilities for the small business to seize business opportunities in an increasingly competitive global context have been seriously restricted by business environments –internal and external environment in DCs that reflects in their management problems.

The need for efficient and effective management of small businesses in DC's requires urgent attention to the general areas and particular or individual factors influencing the overall performance of small business in DCs, as identified in this book and to make adequate recommendations for improvement and desired performance

The general areas and particular or individual factors identified in this book that need to be improved include:

- External environment - policies, institutions, infrastructure, and technical assistance.
- Internal environment - finance, organisation, personnel, marketing, production, owner/manager management skills.

9.2 External Environment

9.2.1 Policy Environment

To improve on policy environment, it is recommended that various governments in DCs should intervene in a number of dimensions. These include:

- Establishing and sustaining a more enabling legal and regulatory environmental framework for small business promotion and development.
- Harmonizing micro and macro small business policies at different levels.
- Employing targeted small business policies.
- Simplifying existing bureaucratic and administrative requirements for small business.
- Improving support for private sector participation in policy making decisions, including institutional activities for small business.
- Improving research and documentation on small business.
- Ensuring steady political, economic and socio-political environment that will encourage in small business development.
- Ensuring efficiency of transfer and the use of the training programme and knowledge required policy and programmes for small business.
- Initiating and enhancing enterprise culture.

Promoting and sustaining efficient, and performing small firms in DCs is likely to be achieved certainly by establishment of the more needed enabling legal and regulatory environment for small business by existing and future governments in DCs. Every government in DCs interested in the promotion of efficient and effective small business should review existing legal and regulatory environment in relation to suitability to small business promotion and development, so they do not inhibit or obstruct small business performance.

The legal environment is the dimension of the general environment that spells out the legal requirement and associated issues, a business need to consider and adhere to, while carrying out business in a given business environment. This could be discussed under the following:

- Legal systems.
- Government legislations and regulations.
- Business laws and regulation.
- Employment laws and regulations.
- Operational, strategic and intellectual legal issues.
- Implications for managers.

Legal system of a country refers to the rules, or laws, that regulate behaviour, along with the processes by which the laws are enforced, and through which redress for grievances are obtained.

The legal system of a country is of immense importance to managers because, it provides the legal framework that regulates business practices, define the manner in which business transactions are to be conducted or executed, and set down the rights and obligations of those involved in business transactions. The legal environment is important for entrepreneurship as the law constitutes the "rules of the game" for business activity. Entrepreneurs need to identify the legal issues in their business environment that could constitute strategic or operational benefits or threats to the new venture.

Operational legal issues in business may be found in areas like:

- Starting up a business.
- Hiring and firing employees.
- Task compliance.
- Making and enforcing contracts.
- Labour relations.
- Going under and getting out.

Strategic legal issues may also be found in areas like:

- ✓ Product safety and liability.
- ✓ Marketplace behaviour.
- ✓ Product origin and local content.
- ✓ Legal jurisdiction.
- ✓ Arbitration.
- ✓ Property rights.

Legal issues relating to Intellectual property may be found in areas like; abuse or neglect of International property rights.

In a legal sense, the term property refers to a resource over which an individual or business holds a legal title- that is a resource that it owns.

Resources include land, buildings, equipment, capital etc. Property rights also refer to the legal rights over the use to which a resource is put, and over the use made of any income that may be derived from that resource.

It should be recognised that without effective property right protection, businesses and individuals run the risk that the profits from innovative new venture effort will be expropriated, either by criminal elements or by state.

Property rights can be violated in many ways. This could be through private action- theft, privacy, blackmail, and the like by private individuals or groups. It could also be through public action and corruption - the extortion of income or resources from property holders by public officials, such as politicians and government bureaucrats. Entrepreneurs can protect intellectual property through: Patent, Copyrights, Trademarks, etc.

Improving policy environment for small business in DCs also requires that government should reduce the bureaucratic overhead for small firms to make life easier for them. Macro- economic policies that reduce level of bureaucracy facing small business- through shift from direct tax to indirect tax, reduction to level of personal tax, simplified taxation system of self assessment. There is the good news that the new Companies and Allied Matters Act (CAMA) bill has been passed by the Nigeria senate on 15th of May 2018, to help improve ease of doing business in Nigeria and particularly, reduce bottlenecks associated with bureaucracy for small and medium enterprises.

Despite the good news coming from Nigeria, there is however the need to improve macro- economic policies that create new market opportunities for small business in DCs. Such policies that encourages strategic and sub-contracting between small and large business should be be improved for example, by asking government departments and agencies to encourage and support small businesses through their procurement strategies and contracts.

Governments in DCs should also give special attention to harmonizing micro and macro small business policies at different levels, and creating a stable and favourable business environment for small business promotion and development in areas of low rate of inflation, stable exchange rate, low interest rate etc.

At the national level, every government in DCs interested in promotion of efficient and effective small business activities should review existing macro-economic policies in terms of suitability to small business activities, so they do not inhibit or obstruct the development of small business. As such, small business policies should be integrated into the national economic policy and planning framework of the government, so that the needs and problems of this sector are always in the minds of policy makers and administrators, who form and implement policies.

The most effective way of integration small business policy with the overall national economic policy should be through periodic re-evaluation of existing policies. Such re-evaluation is best conducted on regular (e.g. annual) bases involving representatives of all the public and private sectors including external assistance donors and agencies. This will help to identify constraints in time so as to apply adequate corrections.

It is also important that policies on small business promotion and development are targeted. At the sectoral level, governments should focus on selected small businesses in DCs, those with the biggest potential for modernization and growth, rather than on all small businesses, some of which are bound to perish. This approach would allow for better allocation and use of resources.

The performance of small businesses in DCs will also improve if governments in DCs take time to develop and implement policies that assist small businesses secure market opportunities overseas through policy alliances overseas, access to overseas trade missions, provision of necessary information on international trade opportunities and advice, etc.

Policy environment for small business promotion and development can also can be improved through government support for private sector participation in policy making decisions, including institutional activities. Purely public sector institutions meant to support the small business have shown many deficiencies, which could be overcome by consultation or partnership with the private sector. So, while government should continue to play a leading role, the small business sector will benefit more from the co-operative efforts of both the public and private sectors. In UK for example, there is a strong private sector participation in small business promotions and development. There are private individuals, institutions and agencies involved in small business investments and advisory programmes and projects. For example The Business Clubs are regional organisations found all over UK. They are made up of businesses in the area and particularly useful for new firms. Often speakers from the Inland Revenue or insurance companies are invited to speak on tax, VAT, grants, etc. A list of members is available and businesses provide advice to each other, and certain amount of inter-trading also takes place. Business clubs also help new firms to make needed initial contacts in various business areas that may help them reduce some risks when initiating a business venture. Trade Associations such as British Travel Agents or the Booksellers Association provide specialist trade advice about certain types business or industry to potential small business owners. The Consumers' Association - Which? is a brand name used by the Consumers' Association, a registered charity and a company limited by guarantee which is based in the UK and exists to promote informed consumer choice in the purchase of goods and services by testing products, highlighting inferior products or services, raising awareness of consumer rights and offering independent advice. The associations also help provide specialist trade advice about certain types business or industry to potential small business owners, and publishes the magazine "Which? That includes "Guide to Starting your own business". There are also Business Links that offer variety of help to businesses, such as technical assistance. It is an independent body. They operate as an independent body that provide funds for businesses. The small business owner also can access a wide range of information and advice through the Business Links. Business Links advisers work with local businesses to identify growth opportunities to develop essential support package as may be needed. Business Links are intended to be self supporting as businesses are expected to pay for many of the services received. They aim particularly to help existing small business with the will to grow especially, small firms usually with 10 to 200 employees. Venture Capital Trusts (VCTs) who are vehicles for private individuals to invest in smaller firms in UK. VCTs offer adventurous investors the chance to invest in small firms to help them grow. They help investors look after their wealth and foster the growth of UK businesses.

As this is a crucial area, the government offers generous tax breaks to VCT investors. Investors in VCTs benefit from tax relief on income tax from dividends and capital gains tax on disposal of shares. There are also Venture capitalists. The entrepreneur can raise loan capital from a venture capitalist. Venture capitalists are specialist organisations that tend to cater for businesses, especially the small business, who have difficulties in raising funds from conventional sources. They provide funds for small firms that appear to have some potential but are considered risky by conventional sources of finance. Business Angels are also a source of loan capital for entrepreneurs. Business Angels are individuals who invest money often in exchange for equity stake - either individually or together with a small group of friends, relatives or business associates. Most of their investments are in start-ups or early stage of business expansions. There are several reasons people become Business Angels - excitements of the gamble involved, being part of a new developing business, tax relief offered by the government, investment opportunities for unused income, such as retired business people and lottery winners.

Small businesses in DCs also need to take advantage of advice from experienced individuals. Advice from individuals can come from people who have started their own business and have gone through the process of setting up and running a small business successfully or from professionals in the field such as an accountant – who can give advice on accounts, bookkeeping, taxation etc; a solicitor - who can give advice on the legal requirements of the business; a business consultant – who can give advice on how to start, run the business, etc.

Improving the data base on the small business in DCs is also crucial for development of policies and measures conducive for the small business. The government should improve programmes in research and documentation by providing facilities in this respect. Private sector participation will also be very helpful including technical assistance in this respect.

Technical assistance for example, should contribute to the success of government policies and measures through continued government and private sector consultation (in policies, and strategies conducive to the development of small businesses), and also assist in policy and strategy formulation, integration, and harmonization macro-economic policies and incentive measures that will be conducive for the development of small business in DCs Policy making institutions also require intensified technical assistance in this respect.

The importance of adequate and reliable infrastructure for the promotion and development of small business in any economy especially in developing economies cannot be overemphasized. Government is expected to improve the condition and availability of infrastructure. In this case, there is need for an increase in policy attention on the importance of infrastructure in small business development in DCs.

Ensuring that there is steady political, economic and socio-political environment by governments in DCs will in doubt encourage promotion and development efforts in small business. It is clear that steady policies through a steady government would also help to carry out steady policy measures, which are normally disturbed by the frequent changes in governments in many DCs. It is not only the economic, but also the political environment which stimulates or hampers small business development. Generally, entrepreneurs do not take the risk to make investment in an unstable or unsteady government. Therefore, the need for a stable political environment in DCs cannot be overemphasized.

For efficiency of transfer and the use of the training programme and knowledge required, policy and programmes implementation has to be improved to provide the necessary environment that could help facilitate the highly needed training programmes. For example, it has been identified that wrong implementation of policies and programmes (e.g. SAP in many African countries) have contributed to input problems like raw materials, spare parts, etc.

Apart from macro-economic factors introduced, the development or enhancement of a number of micro-economic activities in terms of hard and soft schemes, innovative policies, grants and awards, incubator units or offices, enterprise zones - directed to individual new venture and small firms - can also help create enterprise culture. Governments can introduce these to improve enterprise culture (correcting market failures), intended to help new ventures and existing small firms acquire skills, and resources they need to survive and grow. They can also be used to strengthen economic competitiveness in an economy, by creating a healthy, vibrant business sector which the entrepreneur is part of.

Hard support and soft support schemes can be provided by the government to encourage new ventures and entrepreneurs. Hard support schemes may include tangibles such as money, building, equipment etc. and varies (provision of finance, physical infrastructure, etc). Soft support schemes may include intangibles such as education, know-how, etc, - that may come in forms of training, advice, consultancy, helping potential small business entrepreneurs to acquire general business skills and expertise in business specialist subjects such as accounting, taxation, legal issues, marketing and exporting, etc. These may be provided through the education system or through specialist organisations in the public and private sector. Both hard and soft support can be provided nationally, regionally, locally and can be targeted at all stages in the life cycle of a small firm. They are intended to raise awareness of the opportunities for self employment, stimulate the birth of new small ventures, and facilitate survival and growth. Throughout Europe and USA the Chamber of Commerce has played an active role in this context and new technology sectors are normally encouraged and promoted. However, developing countries usually promote business efficiency in non technology sectors such as retail. Overall, many governments are subsidising or paying in full for these services for small firms to enjoy since many entrepreneurs are either unwilling or unable to pay for management consulting or for training and consulting, Governments can also introduce macro policies to support innovation in technology. Such policies can be targeted at universities and government research departments or centres, and are intended to encourage commercialisation of research. Grants and awards can also be used to focus on existing entrepreneurs and small business intended to stimulate new product and process development through grants and awards.

In general, governments in DCs should initiate and enhance policies that developed culture of enterprise. There is no agreed definition of the concept of an enterprise culture. However, the enterprise culture might be conceived as one, requiring individuals, groups and organisations to take responsibility for their own destiny (ownership), rather than been dependent on others. It is about being dependent on one-self. It is about a proactive culture that is encourages initiating, doing, achieving new ventures or enterprises. Citizens need to develop a greater sense of enterprise and self help. In this sense, they are required to take ownership of their own destiny- for the benefit of themselves, their families and their countries and even the world. It should no longer practicable for them to rely on others or governments to provide them with wealth, jobs, etc. - they have to rely on themselves, so they have to empower themselves. DCs therefore need people or citizens, who see opportunity, create and build, initiate, and achieve than ever,

Every individual in DCs needs to become more responsive, having to innovate more quickly, in order to compete, and having to become more agile. This is an issue in DCs. It should be a national priority for governments in DCs to release and support the skills of men and women who can envision and push innovation. Entrepreneurs, entrepreneurship and small business are now seen as the best instrument for change, and the world is demanding both entrepreneurs and more of entrepreneurs and small business, as they provide economic dynamism and growth.

9.2.2 Institutional Framework

In addition to improving policy environment, the institutional framework for small business in DCs can also be improved in terms of their capacity to deliver efficient services to small business in DCs, which demand re-examination and re-assessment of the existing institutions in line with their prevailing problems.

With respect to improving institutional efficiency through technological diffusion or adaptation, the UNIDO technical assistance can adequately support governments in DCs in to achieve this Endeavour, and should intensify its activities in this regard.

Governments in DCs also need to improve in the provision of infrastructural facilities as enabling factor for successful small business promotion and development. The small business is always handicapped by lack of resources and poor infrastructure and this is an added burden. Public /private partnership will go a long way to assist the small business in areas where adequate infrastructure is lacking, for example, in developing or improving existing industrial estates, developing incubator units or offices. Many countries in the world are now developing incubator units or offices and science parks intended to create clusters of new small businesses with similar needs and interests. The aim is to help small businesses solve the problem with office space, and create an environment that encourages and foster entrepreneurship, new venture development and sustainability. In such environment, small businesses can benefit from economies of proximity and association as well as the provision of common support and advisory. The Enterprise Zone is a tax free haven where government bureaucracy is kept to the minimum particularly with respect to land use planning regulation.

The introduction of Enterprise Zone is modelled on Hong Kong, The creation of Enterprise Zones is now becoming popular in many countries as a specialist form of micro support directed to entrepreneurship and small business development – Where they do not have to pay local authority rates and are exempt from certain regulatory restrictions, in particular planning constraints. Some countries use it to encourage export promotion.

Due to their limited resources, small businesses in DCs should take the advantage of acting together in co-operation or as a group. These points to the direction of resource concentration in specific areas of strengths. If small businesses in DCs can develop the spirit of working together in groups, they would be able to reduce most of their dependency on existing institutions and management problems. They can also achieve economy of scale and scope which large scale businesses enjoy. This approach of acting in co-operation or as a group would facilitate their entrepreneurial ability by enhancing:

- ✓ Availability of necessary group facilities and less dependency on outsiders, encouraging flexibility.
- ✓ Collaborative inter-firm relationship.
- ✓ Strong and faster information network.
- ✓ Possibility of sharing ideas and resources.

By using available resources together collectively and efficiently, individual small business acting as a group will have the opportunity of investing and having access to expensive equipment, which could be individually expensive or uneconomical. In addition, all the services that individual large scale industries can call internally – design, purchasing, market research, distribution etc, - can also be provided collectively, as well as fuller use of this capacity that secures greater efficiency and lower unit cost. Also, when using resources together and organized properly, all small businesses involved can achieve economies of scale and scope together. This refers to the relative ease and cost and scope of responding to changing production and marketing requirements. By these means, they are helped to be strong in price dictated type of competitive advantage, that is to say, they are able to offer products which are differentiated from lower price alternatives by features which are now very much in demand – quality products – quickly and efficiently.

It is argued, based on some very valid experiences in Europe, that the limited resources and the consequent weakness of small businesses is because of the relative powerlessness of these enterprises to influence markets and policies. To a significant extent this could be overcome, by grouping of small businesses within the same sectors – creating "industrial districts". Industrial districts (sometimes referred to as clusters) can provide the physical framework for groupings, leading to integration through inter-firm relations. Gradually, as the group concentration expands and more and more small businesses with similar products are attracted to the area, backward and forward linkages also develops, as well as special services to cater for needs of the small firms in the industrial districts. In Europe for example, such "industrial districts" have led to some of the small businesses in these districts to linking themselves together through strong networks, based on array of inter – firm relation. These linkages, together with the close geographical proximity to each other, enhance the division of labour among firms and have led to increased cooperation between them and the spread of ideas and technical innovation. Backward and forward linkages between small businesses and in some cases with larger firms in the vicinity, have sometimes even led to the joint manufacture of various products. The location of small businesses in a cluster has resulted over the course of time in much closer working (and social) relations and greater mutual trust between the businesses. It is understood that historical and social forces have in most cases been the driving factor in the growth of the "clustering". The spontaneous character of the movement of small businesses to the "industrial districts" has generally given its development a dynamism lacking in several of the planned "industrial estates", "science and technology parks" and "incubators". However, these planned forms of location and relocation of small businesses may have greater success potential when based on existing districts or clusters. They then can serve both as a way of promoting new small business start-ups or relocation of suitable occupants from outside the cluster, and/or firms from within the "district" undergoing modernization and expansion. It is important to recognize that it will be a mistake to base small business support exclusively on the cluster approach. Governments in DCs also need to offer help to dynamic viable small businesses with important social and economic potential that for one reason or another are not located within. a cluster

Large organisations also have their role in creating culture of enterprise in a society or country. They can do this by forming local partnerships between themselves and the small firms in their region. This can involve helping small firm suppliers/contractors through the supply chain by creating strategic alliances or preferred supplier partnerships. They can also sponsor various initiatives intended to promote the creation and development of small enterprises, play important role in the establishment and management of local enterprise agencies as discussed earlier and established schemes to establish new businesses. For example, the British Coal established initiatives (British Steel plc and British Coal Enterprise Ltd) to assist people in creating new ventures in areas affected by losses in their industry. The assistance took the form of loans, managed workspaces, training and advice, etc.

Small firm networks and alliances developed in the private sectors can also promote culture of enterprise. This will help create links with large organisations that are important. It will also help link the formal and informal networks. The help and guidance received from both formal network (banks, accountants, lawyers) and the informal networks (family, friends, business contacts) will influence the nature of the small firm's ability to identify, cultivate and manage a network partnership that is an essential condition for survival and success.

Not for profit sector can also contribute to institution building by helping to increased social awareness and enlightenment in enterprise. The result can create a whole range of initiatives, including programmes to assist different sectors of the population in establishing their own business and/or finding employment in small enterprises. In UK for example, non-for –profit initiatives like Instant Muscle has been able to provide young manual workers with basic management skills. Project Full Employ has also helped minority group members set up their own business or find employment. Livewire and the Prince Youth Business Trust have all provided finance for promoting new businesses operated by young people.

9.2.3 UNIDO Technical Assistance

On technical assistance by UNIDO, the impact of this assistance cannot be fully realized unless the encountered project management problems are not treated effectively.

Problems have been located in the design, implementation and follow-up of projects.

On projects design, problems in identification and feasibility studies have been observed. Good and thorough identification missions before project design would help avoid problems in this stage and those frequently encountered in later stage s of the project cycle.

An important role in identification must be given to local representatives of the recipient country as they should have better insight into the country's policy environment and its institutions. In the complex area of small business development with difficulties in defining target group, and with a complex institutional environment, global identification has to be followed by a more specific host country study, using more host country inputs or agencies.

An identification mission should lay the ground work for a feasibility study by indicating:

- The scope of the target group (if possible alternative choices should be made.
- Nature of the target group.
- Nature of the political and institutional environment related to this target group.
- The availability and quality of host country agencies.

The feasibility study should use the data obtained from the identification to quantify the responding output and realistic objectives within the limits of human and capital resources available for the technical assistance project

For the implementation, technical, human, and capital inputs should be fully analysed before implementation to avoid wrong application or use of inputs.

One of the essential tools of project management is monitoring. All the problems already described, which occur at different project levels, could have been avoided if the project had been effectively monitored from the beginning.

Except for cases where to insist on monitoring would definitely be cost ineffective, there is no valid reason for not monitoring.

The problems and needs of small businesses are not homogeneous for DCs even within one country; thus, support to requests for assistance cannot be standardized. As a neutral body which has access to information and expertise world-wide, taking into consideration its long –standing technical co-operation experience in the field of small business in many countries all over the world, and given its industry and sub-sector specific orientation, UNIDO has opportunity to provide recipient countries with tailor- made integrated support packages (support cocktail).

The ultimate mix of support components will depend on the assessment of the needs of the recipient country and take into consideration existing related national and external support efforts in the sector.

A review of many institutions set up to help the promotion and development of small business concluded that highly centralized organisations were not very effective because such institutions needed strong field links and this required considerable local presence.

Local autonomy of action was essential to create decentralized operations. These decentralized operations however, had to be technically competent and this was a problem. As already mentioned, the recruitment of qualified personnel in some provincial regions was especially difficult. Special training schemes need to be undertaken for persons with suitable qualification and experience and on aptitude for the work and remuneration and reward systems have to provide incentives and motivation.

UNIDO is also well positioned to facilitate the dialogue between small businesses, support institutions and government officials. As an international organisation, it should play an advocacy role regarding global issues such as the integration of women in industrial development and balancing regional disparities.

The UNIDO small business programmes should reflect a multi-disciplinary and cross – divisional approach, serving as an instrument in implementing one of the priority goals of UNIDO and the clients it serves. Team formation and co-operation across boundaries within the organisation can ensure interdivisional complementarities of catalytic inputs, which is commensurate with multidisciplinary nature of their needs.

9.3 Internal Environment

9.3.1 Finance

Access to adequate credit has been identified as the most pressing problem in the area of finance for small firms in DCs.

Following accumulated problems associated with obtaining external finance, especially credit, many small businesses are forced to finance their operations using their own capital, with the shortfall being supplied by relatives, friends or non-institutional sources. This has consequences because their financial requirements cannot be satisfied mainly through savings, borrowing from friends and relatives alone. The weak economic situation in many DCs which is not encouraging individual savings rather, has negatively affects on individual savings. It is therefore, not surprising that many small businesses fail as a result of inadequate financing.

Critical areas that demand an urgent attention by both the private and public sector on improving small business financial situation in DCs include:

- ✓ Interest rate charges.
- ✓ Collateral securities.
- ✓ Record keeping.
- ✓ Attitudes of small business owner/manager towards loans.

These problems call for financial strategies that would help solve them.

They may include:

- Initiating and implementing innovative financing techniques to replace or reduce dependency on collateral.
- Use of business plan.
- Government policies that would encourage the use of a chain of financial instruments to share risks and lending.

- Encouraging institutions providing finance to have strong ties to a particular industry or locality and small business representatives.
- Assisting with identification, formulation and implementation of viable projects as well as in start-up operations through intermediaries (e.g. financial institutions and organisations).
- Use of NGOs.
- Pooling resources together by small businesses by encouraging Savings and Loan associations.
- Use of technical assistance.
- Simplification of loan appraisal and approval procedures.
- Adequate training to increase financial awareness and literacy of small business owner/managers and improve attitudes of small business owners.
- Financial policies and implementation strategies that would encourage the provision of special loans from commercial and government banks to small business.

The governments in DCs have the duty to provide adequate macro-economic policies suitable for small business development, including seeking technical assistance of UNIDO or other organisations.

As already observed, existing financial policies have either been inadequate or weak in their implementation and this calls for technical assistance where very needed and when possible to improve finance literacy and management performance of small firms in DCs.

The basis for assessing risk for allocation of credit needs of small firms should be based on human reliability or consciousness, rather than calculation of the value of a person's assets in case of default. This is the successful innovative financing approach in many advanced countries. This innovative financing approaches that have been observed in advanced countries, that point to the way by which funds can be channeled to small businesses, should be adopted by governments and related agencies involved with small business development in DCs.

Preparing a convincing "business plan" may be the first vital step by a small business owner manager to obtaining financing from these innovative investors, but training is required in management including business planning to prepare them adequately. This training can be acquired from various institutions and individual specialists such as management consultants.

Governments in DCs should try to stress the importance of management consultants which at the moment is not a very popular profession unlike their counterparts in developed economies.

Government should also come up with policies that would encourage the use of financial instruments like credit guarantee, re-discounting, re-financing, risk funds, venture capitalists, business angels, etc. These can be used as a chain of financial instruments - that would provide equity capital, and sharing of risk of lending to small businesses.

It is also suggested that financial resources will be better secured if institutions providing them had strong ties to a particular industry or locality and small business representatives are strongly involved in the lending process. This allows the lender and the borrower to work as a group for a particular purpose, in this case finance. In other words, the whole process will help bring both the small business and the lender closer to each other, improve their experience in finance, especially financial skills, and also increase their personal or group relationship, as well as reliability of parties involved.

An outstanding point here is that working in close ties with the lender (e.g. banks) can create the advantage of personal or group reliability, giving room to the group to come close work closely with each other knowing and understanding each other closely, to act as the guarantor for each other. It is also possible for the group to carry out processing functions with clients, checking the credit worthiness, payment etc, thereby reducing the cost for the bank.

As explained earlier in the book, one of the ways of improving the financial situation of small firms is by assisting them in identifying, formulating, implementing and starting viable projects through intermediaries (e.g. financial institutions and organisations.

One of the pressing problems of financial institutions and organisations in doing this is lack of funds and facilities. In this respect, the use NGOs can be suggested to function as intermediaries (non –governmental, non -profit organisation) to financial institutions or organisation such as banks, and as such would deliver fewer costs for the services rendered to banks as intermediaries. NGOs in this respect would act as intermediaries between small businesses. Since they have advantage of local touch, involving them in the finance system would simplify loan appraisal procedures of the financial organisations. However, for this approach to work there is the need for training of NGOs.

It is also suggested that pooling resources together by small businesses would also to a great extent improve the level of their collateral security

In this respect, programmes that attempt to improve access to finance through pooling of resources or savings (allowing pooling of of risk) is highly recommended for small businesses.

Savings and loan Associations (SLAs) represent a system of pooled savings. Their potential, especially in relation to productive investment has been highly neglected by researchers and policy makers.

Pooling of risks through private efforts, especially the Savings and loan Association (SLAs) have been found to have potential to succeed in the future, especially to become a source of short term loans to small businesses if given more encouragement.

Technical assistance and other training programmes for small business should aim at eliminating these financial limitations in order to improve access to finance to small businesses in DCs.

Technical assistance and other training programmes should also be directed to banks and other financial institutions or agencicies proving funds to small for small business aiming at eliminating reducing bureaucracy and red tape by simplification of loan appraisal and approval procedures.

Technical assistance and other training programmes should also be directed towards providing adequate training to small business owner/managers to increase business financial awareness and literacy and improve attitudes to financial management which has so far been poor or inadequate.

9.3.2 Marketing

There is need for improving making activities of small business in DC by helping to solve marketing problems small businesses encounter as already identified earlier in this book such as:

- Poor perception of what the term marketing meant to small business owner.
- Inadequate resources for indentifying market outlets.
- Problem with distribution channels.
- Problems associated with market environment.
- Problems in acquiring marketing information.
- Problems in acquiring marketing information.
- Problems in selling to the government or the export market.
- Lack of standardized products.
- Difficulties with transportation systems.

Small firms in DCs have marketing challenges due to problems associated with:

- ✓ Poor designs, which are both inefficient and inartistic.
- ✓ Low quality of finished products due to the use of poor quality raw materials.
- ✓ Inadequate machines imported second hand or fabricated locally.
- ✓ Insufficient quality control.
- ✓ Lack of precision due to inadequate equipment and lack of skilled personal.
- ✓ Lack of after sales services.

Small business owner managers simply need extensive training in marketing to reduce or eliminate these problems as identified.

There are small businesses in DCs who have been found to have completely ignored or are reluctant to respect marketing as a business function. Some of the reasons associated with this negative behaviour to marketing activities by small business owner managers are related to poor perception of what the term marketing meant, usually a case of ignorance or lack of interest in marketing. Training programmes should be directed towards developing awareness and understanding of the principles of marketing and relative significance to small business success and performance for the small business owner/manager to take active participation. For example, problems with poor designs can be improved through adequate training in technical design and quality management. Low quality of finished products due to the use of poor quality raw materials can be improved through training material sourcing. The problem with inadequate machines imported second hand or fabricated locally can be improved through technical assistance and financial assistance from UNIDO and other financial sources for technical training to improve quality of machine produced locally and facilitate import of right and adequate machine. The problem of insufficient quality control can be improved through training programmes in Total Quality Management (TQM). The problem of lack of precision due to inadequate equipment and lack of skilled personal can be improved through training in needed technical. Lack of after sales services can also be improved through training in marketing skills and techniques. Also training in marketing areas like advertising and product design, distribution, advertising, pricing, promotion etc, is essential for small business to understand the significance to their business.

It is clear that today's business environment is constantly changing and is a source of threats and opportunities to every business large or small. The performance of a small business therefore, will depend on how well owner/ managers understand the business environment and able take advantage of the opportunities and cope with uncertainties associated with environmental threats. This demands improvement in training in marketing principles and practices provided by existing small business service organisation. To achieve this assistance both from home government and abroad in form of technical assistance need to be improved and service delivery to small business monitored continuously to control standard and performance.

Marketing is a window to the outside world and the small business owner/manager need to understand the benefits from the knowledge and application of marketing in this respect through adequate training. Marketing is always having a long term contribution to a business, although many small business owners tend to think short term and it does combats the small business owner/manager from its entrepreneurial culture.

Since marketing looks at consumer needs, it is likely to help the small business increase its ability to satisfy customers, helping to identify attractive marketing opportunity and assessing small business potential to take advantage of any. In other words, marketing provides a guiding philosophy - for the small business direction and activities.

Many small business owners see marketing as an expensive function to run. This is related to inadequate resources for indentifying market outlets, problems associated with market environment, problems in acquiring marketing information, etc. The few institutional sources of information, where necessary marketing data may be obtained are too expensive for small enterprises and generally, the information available are not specific or tailored to small business needs. Any sale information is therefore obtained usually by chance, and only fragmentarily derived from suppliers, customers, other manufacturers and from personal observations. Altogether, the information available does not form a sufficient basis, even to plan medium-term investment and production levels.

Although good marketing personnel are hard to find and demand higher salaries that they deserve, small business owners in DCs have many options. The small business owner managers can make market research easy by observing things around them. For example, they can evaluate new location by observing vehicles and pedestrian traffic. They can carry out their marketing by themselves (starting in a simple small scale) which is easy and cheap for them. They can obtain market research information by making visit to stores and businesses around them to check on products, facilities and price. Customer information can also received and evaluated by recording how many and what kind of customers shop in their stores at different times. They can also conduct informal survey using small samples that can easily be obtained by them including conducting informal focus group survey of friends or targeted groups by inviting them to launch. They can take advantage of their one man business and personal contacts to talk to customers visiting the business. Small business owner/managers can equally conduct their own simple experiment by changing things and watching its effect. They can also obtain secondary data available to large firms and use them to their own advantage.

It has been identified that small businesses in DCs also have great problems in selling to the government or the export market. The products of many small businesses in the DCs are not standardized and are relatively small in quantity. Their products are therefore restricted to the local market. Relative high production cost low quality of small business products and other expenses make it difficult for small firm to participation in trade fairs and missions abroad and compete.

Although the small business products can be some of the inputs of large scale enterprises, the non standardization of their products restricts their access to national and international markets, so, non-harmonization of the production process of small business continues to restrict their marketing horizons-limiting possibilities of market expansion and steady, guaranteed market. Governments in DCs therefore need to improve opportunities for small business by directing their efforts to helping small firms participate in exports and giving them the right international exposures and financial assistance.

It is important that governments in DCs should try to patronize the small business especially at their early stages of start-ups

As already mentioned governments in DCs should reduce if possible eliminate restrictive bureaucracies like the imposition of certain requirements which small businesses are unable to meet, such as the size of the order or the delivery schedule. They should also give special preference to small business to improve their ability to have access to government contracts and transportation systems and other possible assistance to help reduce or eliminate marketing costs involved in those areas.

9.3.3 Personnel

There is therefore the need to intensify training programmes in personnel management to develop local manpower capability in fabricating and maintaining machinery and equipment as well as managing process and human resources.

Generally, small businesses in DCs are run by entrepreneurs who have little or no education or training. They are also staffed with workers who suffer from the same deficiency. In this area of personnel, local capabilities should be improved. The small business owner/manager needs management training so that he/she can deliver the right personnel training to workers. In many cases, small business owner/managers and employees acquire their training through apprenticeship training which is the most formalized training scheme operated in most DCs. This scheme provides over 50% of employment in small business sector, including the men and women who act as proprietors of small business. It is recommended that the government should help small business in developing apprenticeship programme that is suitable for small business activities as done in developed countries like UK.

Since training is usually carried out by the small business entrepreneurs or senior employees. It is a known fact that a man can only teach what he knows and effectiveness of a teacher in part depends on the teaching facilities at his disposal. Many small business entrepreneurs have little or no formal education. Therefore proper training is required which can be delivered by small business institutions set up in many DCs. For these institutions to be effective, they need government assistance as well technical assistance in developing and delivering of management training to small business.

Most seriously, small businesses in DCs have problems recruiting workers or even keep the good ones. There is also the need to improve working conditions to improve recruitment and retention as many trainees have only drifted to the apprenticeship training system for lack of alternative employment opportunities rather than out of genuine interest to acquire the skills being taught. In consequence, the motivation to learn is low and it is not unusual to see some trainees abandoning their training before the scheduled time. Added to this is the fact that small businesses generally do not have the resources to conduct any formal training programmes or send their workers for out of plant training. In response, attention should be given to these challenges and adequate resources made available to them on time to improve their conditions and management performance.

Workers are generally reluctant to work in small business sector which offer worse pay and inferior terms of working conditions compared to the large ones. For the same reasons, many workers tend to leave the small business as soon as they have acquired a certain level of skill or experience. This problem has grown more acute in countries where there is shortage of skilled manpower. Improving working condition in small firms is a very necessity. This can be done by the small business owner improving financial and non financial incentive through government and private sector partnership and assistance to attract workers to the small business sectors. The small business owner/managers can also introduce and implement personal related incentive programmes and systems such as performance related pay or opportunity for partnership, etc, to attract and retain workers by them developing feelings and sense of ownership and belonging to the small business and its future. To achieve this, personnel management training will be essential for the small business owners.

It could be argued that a good competent group of employees is an essential fact for the success of any business. Finding and keeping good employees is not a matter of luck but rather the result of aggressive recruitment, careful selection, proper training and motivation including thoughtful management. Often because of lack of fund, small businesses are not able to afford the employment and retaining of qualified staff to man their production processes and output. In this case, governments in DCs should try to improve access to funding for small business as already indicated in terms of financing.

The small business is usually managed along personal or family line, without much consideration of competence and performance. It often happens that job and competence are usually considered on private or personal relationship. Among many reasons for problems encountered in this area is the use of family labour especially in strategic positions. Usually family members occupy strategic positions in many small businesses, in order to maintain the needed owner/manager influence or authority. In most cases employment is not based on competence but personal relationship. This usually affects the overall performance of the small scale industry in question. Training programmes should be directed to correct these problems to help the small business owner understand the downside of nepotism and negative impact to performance in the small business.

9.3.4 The Small Business Owner/Manager

As already identified, some of the management problems of the small business have been traced to the small business owner/managers in DCs who share a number of characteristics that have become a source or management problems. To reduced this problem or even eliminate them and achieve management and business performance, the small business owner/managers need management and technical trainings to help them develop and apply essential management skills such as:

- ✓ Conceptual skills.
- ✓ Human relation skills.
- ✓ Technical skills.
- ✓ Entrepreneurial skills.

Small business owner/managers, just like any other managers, need to have conceptual skills. Conceptual skills relate to the cognitive ability of a manager to see the organisation as whole as well the relationship among various parts that make up the organisation. It is a direction or vision skill. It demands a manager's thinking and planning abilities that involve knowing where his/her business fits into the industry and community or environment. It requires the owner/manager to develop the ability to think strategically and take a broad view to see the big picture. Conceptual skills are especially needed by small business owner/managers. As the sole proprietor of the business, he/she must make difficult decisions and need to needed to give the small business the right direction, and should have the ability to perceive the significant elements in situations, and make decision relevant to broad conceptual pattern that will take the small business to the next level.

In addition to conceptual skills, small business owner/managers will no doubt perform well if they can demonstrate effective human relation skills. Human relation skills related to the ability to work with and through other people. It includes the ability to motivate, coordinate, lead, communicate, get along with others and resolve conflicts. Human relation skill allows small business managers recognise the importance of relationship with other people involved in their business, including the ability to express themselves without fear and encourage participation. Efficient human relation skills enable small business owner/managers to unlash energy of those involved them in the business activities.

As explained earlier, many small business owner/managers start-up their firms based on technical skills already acquired. Technical skill is important because this enhances the number and quality of products and service delivery, as technical skill is the understanding of and proficiency in performing specific tasks - that includes master of methods, techniques and equipment involved in specific function, specialised knowledge, analytical skill, competent use of tools and techniques to solve problems.

It is the fact that small firms can quite quickly lose their entrepreneurial momentum as they grow. To prevent this happening, the key is to evolve an organisational structure and style of management that prevents the small business from this limitations by creating an adaptive organisation – an institution capable of facilitating the character of the entrepreneur, namely to perceive and pursue opportunities, and to believe success is possible, and seeking to achieve competitive advantage.

To achieve competitive advantage, the small businesses owner/manager can take advantage of entrepreneurial skills and and peculiar characteristics of small business. It is important to recognise that small businesses have been noted to have peculiar characteristics that are entrepreneurial in nature, and this can be used to achieve competitive performance. Some characteristics that are entrepreneurial attributed to small business are flexibility and adaptability to business environment due to their small size. Becoming a successful small owner/manager therefore, requires a blend of all these skills as described above - conceptual skills, human relation skills, technical skills and entrepreneurial skills. While small business managers should remain entrepreneurial, which relates to small business peculiar characteristics, personal characteristics, or individual attributes, creative thinking, practical skills etc, they also need the use of general business management skills for the small business to go a long way in operations and performance. Some of these skills can come out of training or experience and possibility delivered through training from small business service institutions as well as UNIDO technical assistance.

9.3.5 Production

For small businesses to operate and compete effectively, it is necessary that they should be in the position to produce effectively.

As already identified, one main problems hindering production activities of small business in DCs is the issue of the standard and quality of technology available to them. There is limited availability of technology, most technology available is imported, efforts to reduce this importation of technology have led to the pressure of local sourcing in many DCs. Attempts have therefore been made to produce the required technology internally and one of the most obvious problems that reduce production efficiency of small businesses in DCs is their utilization of traditional technology. However, there is evidence that productivity is relatively low in many small businesses because they still employ traditional method of production which have failed to keep up with the speed of new techniques or modern technology. Lack of necessary fabrication facilities is one of the major reasons behind the low performance of this machinery and equipment, and where the fabricating industries succeed in producing machinery and equipment, these machines lack functioning ability. In addition, lack of foreign exchange further reduced the general possibility of importation and hence the volume of technology available.

Many of these imported machines are used ones and mostly not modern.

Some are even imported in non-working condition with the hope of repair at home. Anything is acceptable, especially in the small scale sector, as they cannot afford quality equipment because of their poor bargaining power. Imported machines also suffer from low efficiency because of a lack of indigenous expertise for their installation, maintenance and repair. In many cases machinery and equipment is idle as there is nobody to repair it. In cases where repairs are done, it is a matter of trial and error and the machines are often breaking down due to improper repairs. Added to this is shortage of spare parts of maintaining or repairing available foreign or local machinery. The services of qualified foreign or local manpower are usually too costly for the small business to afford especially on a regular base.

With view of all these problems mentioned above and faced by many small firms in DCs, the role of technological transfer, diffusion or adaptation has now become an important area of interest for exploitation in the bid to improve small business productive performance in DCs.

To achieve these, small business institutions as well as UNIDO technical assistance projects and programmes need to be improved to enhance efficiency and effectiveness of local institutions in training development and building up local of indigenous expertise in local technology. With the fast rate of technology development in world technology, there are now many possibilities in various countries where technology transfer knowledge can be suitable to small business in DCs can be acquired. However, the choice of technology has to be made according to advice and guidance received from within the country where the machinery or process will be used.

Upgrading technology of small business in DCs is vital for the economic development of the sector and ways have to be exploited to accomplish this.

While improving the management skills and operations of small business owner/manager is important, but without raising or upgrading their technology levels, small businesses will not be able to modernize and expand into efficient competitive business.

Over the past years, a whole range of sectoral centers and research and development institutes have been set up in in many DCs

Many have had little effect in assisting small businesses to upgrade their technology.

Technical service centers set up in many DCs as part of industrial estates face similar fates to the research and development centers.

Many are underutilized or left to decay just like that found in Nigeria as reported by Channel television in 2017 news programme.

The practical implementation of technology upgrading or modernization for small business has too often taken place in the past through the guidance and information provided by machine manufacturer's agents who in many cases have exerted undue influence on the technology (i.e. equipment) purchased and used by small businesses. Rarely has the choice of equipment or technology being influenced by advice from technical or research institutes or technology centers even where they exist.

Much has been written of the need for small business in DCs to use simpler and more "appropriate or intermediate technology" as it has been called. Namely technology that is more labour intensive

There is therefore, need for technological adaptation to suit small business environment and needs in DCs.

Technological adaptation should take into consideration the environment of DCs so as to suit their local use, needs and capabilities in installation, maintenance and repair.

It is clear that the issue of transfer of technology has been recognized by governments and institutions in DCs as an important source of reducing production problems encountered by many small businesses in DCs.

The term "transfer of technology" when referred to DCs, is usually meant to imply transfer of the technology in question from a more advanced country. This may not be the only transfer possible or necessarily the most appropriate.

Research studies have shown that technologies are transferred through a variety of forms:

- ✓ In a serendipitous fashion.
- ✓ Through personal contacts with friends or relatives in the same or in other countries.
- ✓ Through visits undertaken on their own initiative (and expense) by small business entrepreneurs.
- ✓ Through joint ventures with international bodies or firms, etc.

There are a number of recognized formal arrangements for implementing a transfer of technology:

- ✓ Technical assistance agreements.
- ✓ Know – how agreements.

- ✓ Joint ventures.
- ✓ Subcontracting,
- ✓ Licensing.
- ✓ Franchising.

the answer to the question of which of these recognized formal agreements will be most appropriate for the small business in DCs, will depend on particular needs and abilities of the enterprises both at the source and the receiving end.

The "know-how" or technical assistance agreements generally consists of an enterprise, selling technical information usually relating to the design, manufacture, servicing or testing of a product, and would probably involve the sales of drawings, blueprints, specifications and detailed data on the designs of products or parts as well as the equipment and tooling that may be needed to produce the item.

Clearly, this agreement can, and must in some cases, involve a relationship over a longer period and include training of personnel from the receiving enterprise. Although "know-how" and technical assistance agreements are very similar, the latter tends to imply a more "hands-on" arrangement over a wider range and a longer period. However, there are "pitfalls" in such agreements and most small business need advice on choosing the most suitable and economic technology and source of transfer, as well as help to ensure that the enterprise concerned is able and willing to provide all the information and help needed. Such advice and guidance on both the choice of technology and the appropriate provider and the manner of implementation of the agreement, can be provided by private consultants, technical advisory service supported by chamber of commerce and industry, business associations, etc.

As regards other forms of more specific transfer agreements – licensing, joint ventures, franchising – these are generally the main form of technology transfer within the industrialized countries today. However, for DCs, these agreements may present problems.

Licensing agreements requires that the receiving small business and the DCs where it operates, has adequate technical skills to handle the technology involved. However, the more advanced developing countries (e.g. Korea, India, Mexico) all have sufficient technical infrastructure and skills to use licensing agreements effectively and do so, but many LDCs are not in that situation. Licensing also means that the enterprise (for a cash payment- either a lump sum of payment annually, or on occasions royalties per item produced), receive technical details – drawings, specifications etc – regarding manufacture of the product and permission to produce and market the product under an agreed brand name. No capital is contributed by the provider of the license and this is usually a problem but could be solved when a joint venture is set up – a common manufacturing facility whose ownership is shared by both the provider and receiver of the license. However, most small firms in DCs require more than a license to produce; they generally need a more comprehensive "know-how" agreement and/or technical assistance to make a success of the transfer of technology.

Franchising another form of transfer of "know-how" is mostly confined to industrialized countries and most often takes place in service industries. It involves the use of trademarks and rarely the actual transfer of real technology although it often includes some limited technical advice. Until now, it has limited application in DCs.

Sub-contracting has been presented as important way to affect transfer of technology. It is presumed that when a small business carries out order for another firm, usually large but sometimes another small firm, the contracting firm who gives the order provides the "know –how" and technical assistance needed by the subcontractor to carry out the work according to the required quality, price and delivery date.

The firms help their subcontractors with specifications, detailed drawings, designs, tooling and even special production and quality control equipment to do the work.

Further reading

Bacal, R. (2009), Perfect Phases for Managing Your Small Business, NY, McGraw Hill.
Burker, G. (2008), Growing Your Small Business: a handbook for ambitious owner/managers, NY, Routledge.
Byrd, M. (2009), Small Business Management, Boston, McGraw Hill.
Chaston, I. (2009), Entrepreneurial Management in Small Business, London.
Frank, M. (2009), Management of Small Enterprises, NY, Routledge.
Ike, Like (2017), Strategic Management: Concepts & Practices, Xlibris London.
Ike, Luke (2016), Risk Management & Captive Insurance, Xlibris, London.
Ike, Luke (2017), Business Strategy: An Introduction), Xlibris, London
Ike, Luke (2017), International Business: Environments & Operations, Xlibris, London.
Ike, Luke (2017), International Management: Principles & Practices, Xlibris, London.
Ike, Luke. (2016), Management: Principles & Practices, Xlibris, London
Scarborough, N. (2009), Effective Small Business management, Prentice Hall.
UNDP (1990), Project In-depth Evaluation- A Briefing Kit, Central Evaluation Office, New York.
UNDP (2000), Human Development Report, New York.
UNDP Annual Reports, Vienna 1989 – 2000.
UNDP, NaTCAP (2001), Methodology Regional Bureau report for Africa.
UNIDO (1989), Human Resources in Sri Lanka's Industrial UNIDO (2000), Information Report Paper, Vienna, Austria.
UNIDO (1990), Development of the African Traditional Textile Industry Vienna, Austria.
UNIDO (1991 -2000), Country Brief on Agro-related Metal working Industries in LDC in the Asia and Pacific regions.

UNIDO (1993), The Present Situation of Small and Medium Enterprises in Kenya and Tanzania and impact of Structural Adjustment policy

UNIDO (1999), Nigeria Experience on Industrial Project Evaluation, Lagos, Nigeria.

UNIDO: Nigerian Industrial Research Review Series, 1999 -2001.

Weiss, J. (1988), Industry in Developing Countries: Theory, Policy and Evidence, London.

World Assembly of Small Scale Industries, Rabat Symposium on IDDA 1986.

World Bank (1978), Employment and Development of Small Enterprises (sector policy paper), Washington DC.

World Bank (1991), Managing Technical Assistance: reports of the Technical Review Task Force.

Young, A. (1988), Small Scale Business development, New York.

REFERENCES

Akrasanel N et al, (1983), Rural of Farm Employment in Thailand, BangkoK.

Arief, K. (1992), Small Scale Industries and Small Enterprise Credit Programmes in Indonesia.

Baumback, C. (1983), Basic Small Business Management, Prentice Hall, Eaglewood Cliff, New York.

Bautista, R. (1988), Macro Policies and Technology Choice in the Philippines.

Berry, A. (1988), The Relevance of Small Scale Industries New York.

Bolnik, B. (1982), Commercial Credit for Small Business: Bulleting of Indonesia Economic Studies.

Byke and Sengenberger Brusco, S. (1993), Small Firms and the Provision of Real Services.

Cheng Peng Lim (1990), Development of Small Business in Developing Asian Countries, Policy and Institutional Infrastructure Gottingen.

Chee Peng Lim et al, (1984), ASEAN Small and Medium Scale Industries, Kuala Lumpur.

Chee Peng Lim et al, (1988), ASEAN Industrial Cooperation, Perspectives and Alternative Scheme, Asian and Pacific Development Centre Kuala Lumpur.

Chew, S. (1988), Small Scale Firms in Singapore, Oxford University Press.

Child, F. (1990), Small Scale Rural Industry in Kenya, University of California, Los Angeles, African Studies Centre.

Clapham, R.(1985) Small and Medium Enterprise in Southeast Asia, Institute of Southeast Asian Studies Singapore.

Cortes M et al, (1987), Success in Small and Medium Scale Enterprises, The Evidence from Columbia, New York, Oxford University Press

DAC (1991), Development Assistance Committee: Principles for New Orientation in Technical Cooperation.

Dhar, P. (1981), The Role of Small Scale Industries in Indian Economic Development; Institute of Economic Growth, ASIAN Publishing

Gibb, A. (1991), Key Factor of Policy Support for Small Scale and Medium Enterprises, Development Process Gottingen

Geoffrey et al, (1985),Women in Charge, The Experience of the Female Entrepreneur, Allen &Urwin, London

Goh, B. (1989), Survey of Small Scale Industries in ButterwithTown, University of Malaysia.

Haan, C. (1989),The Small Sized Enterprises and Rural Non Farm Employment in Africa, Options for IFAD Involvement, Africa Division.

Haggablade, C. Liedholm, C. Meaf, D. (1989), The Effect of Policy and Policy Reforms on Non-Agricultural Enterprises and Employment in Developing Countries, The Hague, The Netherlands

Harper, M. (1984), Small Business Promotion, Case Studies from Developing Countries, New York.

Ho, K (1985), Information Technology Development for Small and Medium Scale Enterprises in Asia and Japan.

Hunt, R. (1987), Small Enterprise Development and the Voluntary Sector, Neck and Nelson Op cit.

ILO, UNIDO, UNDP, The Netherlands (1988), Development of Rural Small Industrial Enterprise, Lesson from Experience.

ILO (2000), Group Based Savings and Credits for Local Poor, ILO, Geneva.

ILO (1986), The Promotion of Small Scale Industries Vol.1.

ILO (2000), Towards Full Employment Production for Columba, ILO

Industrial Policy for Lagos State, Annual Publication of Lagos State Chamber of Commerce and Industries 1970 – 2016.

Industrial Policy of Nigeria: Policy Incentives and Guidelines and Industrial Framework, Publication of the Lagos Chamber of Commerce and Industries – 1980 – 2016.

Jacobson, L. (1985), Job Creation and Development, The Upjohn Institute, New York.

James Austin (1990), managing in Developing Countries, Strategic Analysis and Operating Techniques

Kaviraj, A. (199), Small na medium Sized Enterprises and European Union.

Kim, C. (1985), A Study on the Technology Development Policy of Small Industry, Korean Economic Study Centre, Seoul.

Kim, K. (1992), Need for Cooperation in Asean Small and Medium Scale Industries.

Koch, M. (1990), Commercial Loans for Small Business Manufacturers in Latin America, Empirical Evidence on Formal Sector Credit in Columbia, Ecuador and Peru.

Kogi, K. 1989), Improving Working Conditions in Small Enterprises in Developing Asia ILO, Geneva.

Konig, W. (1992), Techniques and Criteria for Classifying Small and medium Industries by Size.

Konig, W. (1991), External Financing for Small Scale Enterprises, Gottingen.

Lagos State Industrial Guide: Publication of Lagos State Chamber of Commerce and Industries 1992.

Lagos State Progress Report 2000 – 2017.

Lau, P. (1983), The Role of Small Industries in Singapore's Reconstruction, Singapore

Lelandra De Sive (1989), Development Aid: A Guide to Facts and Figures.

Neck, P. (2000), Small Enterprise Development: Policies and programmes, ILO, Geneva.

NIDB; Nigeria, Industrial Development Bank, Annual Report, 2012 -2016.

O'Connoor, J. (1987), Women in Enterprise: Industrial Development Authority and Office Minister of State for Women's affairs, Dublin.

OECD (1988), Geographical Distribution of Financial Flows to Developing Countries, Paris.

OECD (1988), The Newly Industrialising Countries, Challenges and Opportunity for OECD Countries, Paris.

OECD (1985), Creating Jobs at the Local Level, Paris.

Scarborough, H. (2000), Effective Small Business Management, Columbia,. Ohio

Sharma, S. (1979), Small Entrepreneurial Development in Some Asian Countries, New Delhi.

Shetty, M. (1963), Small Scale and Household Industries in a Developing Economy, Asian Publishing.

Tan, H. (1975), Enterprise System and Economic Development in Singapore, London University.

Teitz, M. (1983), Small Buisness and Employment Growth, University of California, Berkeley, California.

UNDP (2000), Human Development Report, New York.

UNDP, NaTCAP (2001), Methodology Regional Bureau report for Africa.

UNDP (1990), Project In-depth Evaluation- A Briefing Kit, Central Evaluation Office, New York.

UNDP Annual Reports, Vienna 1989 – 2000.

UNIDO (1991 -2000), Country Brief on Agro-related Metal working Industries in LDC in the Asia and Pacific regions.

UNIDO (1990), Development of the African Traditional Textile Industry Vienna, Austria.

UNIDO (2000), Effectiveness of Industrial Estates, Vienna, Austria.

UNIDO (1989), Human Resources in Sri Lanka's Industrial Development: The Current and Prospective Contribution of Women Vienna Austria.

UNIDO (2000), Information Report Paper, Vienna, Austria.

UNIDO (1999), Nigeria Experience on Industrial Project Evaluation, Lagos, Nigeria.

UNIDO: Nigerian Industrial Research Review Series, 1999 -2001.

UNIDO (1988), Reports on First Consultation of Small Scale Industries Vienna, Austria.

UNIDO (1993), Small Scale Industries Review Publication Vienna, Austria.

UNIDO (1991), Stimulating Rural Small Industries in Developing Countries, Working on Industrial Development in LDCs Towards an Industrial Action Plan, Vienna, Austria.

UNIDO (1974), Sub-contracting for Modernising Economics, New York.

UNIDO (1990), Summary of 14 Case Studies on the State of Manufacturing Industries with Emphasis on Food Processing Industry.

UNIDO (1993), The Present Situation of Small and Medium Enterprises in Kenya and Tanzania and impact of Structural Adjustment policy

Weiss, J. (1988), Industry in Developing Countries: Theory, Policy and Evidence, London.

World Assembly of Small Scale Industries, Rabat Symposium on IDDA 1986.

World Bank (1978), Employment and Development of Small Enterprises (sector policy paper), Washington DC.

World Bank (1991), Managing Technical Assistance: reports of the Technical Review Task Force.

Young, A. (1988), Small Scale Business development, New York.

Baumol, W. J. (1967) Business Behaviour, Value and Growth, Harcourt Brace.

Bolton Report (1971), Report on the Commission of Enquiry on Small Firms, Cmnd 4811 HMSO.

Burns, P. et al, (1996), Small Business and Entrepreneurship, Second Edition, Macmillan Business.

Cannon, T. (1991), Enterprise Creation, Development and Growth, Butterworth – Heinemann.

Casson, M. (1982), The Entrepreneur; An Economic Theory, Martin Robertson.

Churchill N.C. and Lewis V. L. (1983), The Five \Stages of Small Business Growth, Harvard Business Review, May/June 1983.

Curran, J. et al, (2000), The Survival of the Small Firm, Gower.

Davis J. R. and Kelly, M. (1972), Small Firms in the Manufacturing Sector, Report of the committee of Enquiry on Small Firms, Cmnd4811, HMSO.

Ganguly, T. (1983) UK Small Business Statistics and international comparisons, Harper & Row.

Kakabadse, A. (1983), The Politics of Managing Growth.

O'Farrel, F. N, (1986), Entrepreneurs and Industrial Change, Irish Management Institute

Ray, G. H. And Hutchinson, P. J. (1983), The Financing and Financial Control of Small Enterprise Development, Govern.

Stanworth, J, et al, (1991), The Small Firm in the 1990s, Paul Chapman

Storey, D. et al, (1987), The Performance of \New Firms, Croom Helm.

Storey, D. J. (1982), Entrepreneurship and the new Firm, Croom Helm

Utton, M. A. et al, Small Business Theory and Policy, The Action Society, Croom Helm

Wynarczyk, P. K. Et al, (1993), The Managerial Labour Market in the Small firm Sector, Rutledge.

Adrian, Palmer (2004), Principles of Marketing (4th Edition), Oxford University Press.

Alan, Anderson (2004) Economics) (4th Edition), Causeway Press.

Alderfer, C. (1972), Existence, Relatetedness and Growth;Human needs in organisational settings, Free Press, New York.

Alexander, D.and Nobes, C. (2004), International Introduction to Financial Accounting, Financial Times, /Prentice Hall, Harlow.

Alvesson, M. and Wilmott, H. (1996), Making Sense of Management, Sage, London.

Andersen, T. (2000), Strategic Planning, autonomous and corporate performance, London.

Anderson, T. and Metcall, H. (2003), Diversity; Slacking up the evidence of Executive briefing, Chartered Institute of Personnel and Development, London.

Anold, J. Hope, T. (1995), Financial Accounting (2nd Edition), Financial Times/Prentice hall, Hemel Hempstead.

Ansoff, F, H, (1965), Corporate Strategy, Pengioum, London.

Arthur, W. (19 85) Risk management and insurance, (5th Edition) London press

Bandara, A. (1997), Self Efficacy; The Exercise of Control, Freeman, New York.

Barile A. (1983)The captive insurance company: An emerging profit centre. Best review in property, and casualty insurance, 7th Edition New York.

Bass, P. (2000), Changing The Culture of a Hospital From Hierarchy to Netwooked Community, Pblic Administration London.

Batt, P. (2000), Managing Customer Services: Human Resource Practices London.

Bearshaw, et al (2004) Economics: A student's Guide (5th edition), Pitman Pub;ishing.

Becker, B. Huselid, M. The Human Resource Scorecard, Harvard Business School Press, Boston.

Bucanan, D. and Badham, R. (1999), Power, Politics and Organizational Change: Wining the turf game, Sage, London.

Bucanan, D. and Bobby, R. [1992], The Expertise of the Change Agent, Prentice Hall International, Hamel Hempsted.

Bucanan, D. and Huczynski, A.A [2004], Organizational Behaviour: An introductory text [50th edn], Financial Times/Prentice Hall, Harlow.

Burnes, B. [1996], Managing Change, Pitman, London.

Burns, J.M. [1978], Leadership, Harper & Row, New York.

Burns, T. [1961], 'Micropolitics: mechanisms of organizational change', Administrative Science Quarterly, vol.6, no.3, pp. 257 – 281.

Burns. T. and Stalker, G.M. [1961], The Management of Innovation, Tavistock, London.

Butt, J. [1971], Robert Owen: Prince of cotten spinners, David &Charles, Newton Abbott.

Cairncross, F. [2001], The Death of Distance 2.0: How the communications revolution will change our lives, Orion, London.

Campbell, A. [1997], 'Stakeholder: the case in favour', Long Range Planning, vol. 30, no.3, pp. 446 – 449.

Camuffo, A., Romano, P. and Vinelli, A. [2001], 'Back to the future: Benetton transforms its global network', MIT Sloan Management Review, vol. 43, no. 1, pp. 46 – 52.

Cannon, T. [1996], Basic Marketing: Principles and practice [4th edn], Cassell, London.

Cappelli, P. [2000], 'Managing without commitment', Organizational Dynamics, vol. 28, no. 4, pp. 11 – 25.

Carlson, S. [1951], Executive Behaviour, Stromberg Aktiebolag, Stockholm.

Carr, N.G. [2004], 'In praise of walls', MIT Sloan Management Review, vol. 45, no. 3, pp. 268 – 295.

Carroll, A. (1999), 'Corporate social responsibility'- Business and Society, Vol. 38, pp. 268 – 295.

Caster A. (1984), Handbook of risk management,- London Harron handbooks.

Catterick, P. [1995], Business Planning for Housing, Chartered Institute of housing, Coventry.

Certo SL et al (2007) Modern Management Concerts and Skills (11th Edition) Prentice Hall.

Chaffey, D. [ed.] [2003], Business Information Systems [2nd edn], Financial Times/Prentice Hall, Harlow.

Champy, J. and Nohria, N. [1996], Fast Forward, Harvard Business School Press, Cambridge, MA.

Chandler, A. (1962), Strategy and Structure, MIT Press, Cambridge, MA.

Chapman, D. and Cowdell, T. (1998]), New Public Sector Marketing, Financial Times Management, London.

Chen, M. [2004], Asian Management System, Thomson, London.

Cherns, A. [1987], 'The principles of sociotechnical design revisited', Human Relations, vol 40, no. 33, pp. 153 – 162.

Cherysalides, G.A.D. and Kale, J.H. [1993], An Introduction to Business Ethics, Chapman & Hall, London.

Child, J. [1972], 'Organizational structure, environment and performance: the role of strategic choice', Sociology, vol. 6, pp.1 – 22.

Child, J. [1984], Organisation: A guide to problems and practice [2nd edn], Harper & Row, London.

Chow, I. (1994), 'An opinion survey of performance appraisal practice- in Hong Kong and the People's Republic of China', Asia Pacific Journal of Human Resources, vol. 32, pp. 62 – 79.

Christensen, C.M. and Raynor, M.E. [2003], The Innovator's Solution, Harvard Business School Press, Boston, MA.

CIPD [2002], Pensions and HR's Role, Charted Institute of Personnel and Development, London.

Clarke, F.L. [2003], Corporate Collapse: Accounting, regulatory and ethical failure, Cambridge University Press, Cambridge.

Clutterbuck, D. [1994], The Power of Empowerment, Kogan Page, London.

Coggan, P. [2002], The Money Machine, Penguin, Harmondsworth.

Cole G A (2004) Management Theory and Practice (6th Edition) Thomson

Cooke, B. [2003], 'The denial of slavery in management studies',- Journal of management Studies, vol. 40, no. 8, pp. 1895 – 1918.

Cooke, S. And Slack, N. [1991], Making management Decisions [2nd edition], Prentice Hal Hemel Hempstead.

Coombs, R. and Hull, R. [1994], 'The best or the worst of both worlds: BPR, cost reduction, and the strategic management of IT',paper presented to the OASIG seminar on Organizational Change, London, September.

Cornfield, R. [1999], Successful Interview Skills, Kogan Page, London.

Cravens, D.W. [1991], Strategic Marketing [3rd edn], Irwin, Chicago, IL.

Critchley, W. and Casey, D. [1984], 'second thoughts on team building', Management Education and Development vol. 15, no 2, pp. 163 – 175.

Crosby, P. [1979], Quality is Free, McGraw-Hill, New York.

Cusumano, M.A. and Nobeoka, K. [1998], Thinking Beyond Lean, the Free Press, New York.

Cusumano, M. [1997], 'How Microsoft makes large teams work like small teams', MIT Sloan Management Review, vol. 39, no.1, pp. 9 – 20.

Cyert, R. and March, J.G. [1963], A behavioral theory of the firm, Prentice Hall, Englewood cliffs, NJ.

D Stokes (2006) Small Business Management (4th Edition) Continuum

Daft, R. A. (2010,) New Era of Management (9th Edition) South Western.

Daft, R.L. [2000], Management [5th edn], The Dryden Press, Fort Worth, TX.

Daniels, J.D. and Radebaugh, L.H. [1998], International Business [8th edn], Addison-Wesley, Reading, MA.

Davenport, T.H. [1998], 'Putting the enterprise into enterprise system', Harvard business review, vol. 76, no. 4, pp. 121 – 132.

David Boddy (2012_essentials of Management, A coincise Introduction

David, B. (2012), Essentials of Management, A coincise Introduction, Pearson Education, Prentice Hall.

Davis, K. [1960], 'Can business afford to ignore social responsibilities?' California management review, vol. 2, no. 3, pp, 70 – 76.

Davis, K. [1971], Business Society and Environment: social power and social response, McGrew Hill, New York.

Day G. (1985) Strategic market planning, the pursuit of competitive advantage

De wit, B. And Meyer, R. [2004], strategy: process, content and context, and international perspective, international Thomas Business, London.

Deal, T.E. and Kennedy, A.A. [1982], corporate Culture: the rites and rituals of corporate life, Addison-wesley, Reading, MA.

Delaney, J.T. and Huselid, M.A. [1996], 'the impact of human resource management practices on perceptions of organizational performance' Academy of management journal, vol. 39, no. 4, pp. 949 – 969.

Delmar, F. and Shane, S. [2003], 'Does business planning facilitate the developomet of new ventures?', strategic management journal, vol. 24, no. 12, pp. 1165 – 1185.

Deming, W.E. [1988], out of the crisis, Cambridge University Press, Cambridge.

Dent, C.M. [1997], the European Economy: the global context, Routledge, London.

Department of trade and industry [1996], the rewards of success: flexible pay systems in Britain, DTI, London.
Dibb, S., Simkin, L., Pride, W.M. and Ferrell, O.C. [1997], marjeting: concepts and strategies [4th edn], Houghton Mifflin, New York.
Dicken, P. [1992], global shift: the internationalisation of economic activity, PCP, London.
Dimbleby, R. and Burton, G. [1992], more than words: and introduction to communication [2nd edn], Routledge, London.
Dobson, P. Starkey, K. Richards, J. [2004], Strategic management issue and cases, Blackwell, Oxford.
Domasio, A.R. [2000], The Feeling of What Happened, Heinemann, London
Donaldson, L. [1996], For positive organization theory, Sage, London.
Donaldson, L. [2001], The contingency theory of organization, Sage, London.
Drucker, P.F. [1954], The practice of management, Harper, New York.
Drucker, P.F. [1985] Innovation and entrepreneurship, Heinemann, London
Drucker, P.F. [1999], Butterworth- Heinemann, (2nd edition)Oxford.
Drummond, H. [1996] escalation in decision-making, Oxford university Press, Oxford.
Drury, C. [2004], management and cost accounting, Thomson learning, London.
Druskat, V.U. and Wheeler, J.V. [2004], 'how to lead a self-managing team' MIT, Sloan management Review, vol. 45, no.4, pp. 65 – 71.
Dutta, S. Segev, A. [1999], 'Business transformation on the internet' European management journal, vol. 17, no. 5, pp. 44 – 476.
Dutton, J.E., Dukerich, J.M. and Harwuail, C.V. [1994],'organizational images and member identification', administrative science quarterly, vol. 39, no. 2, pp. 239 – 263.
Economist intelligence unit [1992], making quality work: lessons from Europe's leading companies, economist intelligence unit, London.
Egan, J. and Wilson, D. [2002], private business – public battleground, Palgrave, Basingstoke.

Elliot, B. And Elliot, J. [2003], financial accounting and reporting [6th edn], Financial Times/Prentice Hall, Harlow.

Engel, J. Kollatt, D. and Blackwell, R. [1978], Consumer behaviour, Dryden Press, Boston.

Equal opportunities commission [1999], "facts about women and men in Great Britain", EOC, Manchester.

Ezzemel, M. Lilley, S. and Wilmott, H. [1994], 'the new organization and the managerial work", European management jounal, vol.12, no. 4, pp. 454 – 461.

Fayol, H. [1949], General and Industrial Management, Pitman, London. General and industrial management, Pitman, London.

Feigenbaum, A.V. [1993], Total quality control, McGrew-Hill, New York.

Fenton, E. M. and Pettigrew, A.M. [2000],'theoretical perspectives on new forms of organization', in A.M. Pettigrew and E. Fenton [eds.], the innovating organization, sage, London.

Fieldler, F.E. and House, R.J. [1994],'Leadership theory and research: a report of progress', in C.L. Cooper and I.T. Robertson [eds.], key reviews of managerial psychology, Wiley, Chichester.

Finkelstein, S. [2003], Why smart Executives fail: and what you can learn from their mistakes, penguin, New York.

Fleishman, E.A. [1953], the description of supervisory behaviour, journal of applied psychology, vol. 37, no. 1, pp. 1 – 6.

Flores, S.L and Pearce, S.L. [2000], the use of an expert system in the M3-competition, international jounal of forecasting, vol. 16, no. 4, pp. 485 – 493

Flynn, N. [2002], P ublic Sector Management [4th edn], Financial Times/Prentice Hall, Harlow.

Fogel, R.W. [1989], without consent or contract: the rise and fall of American slavery, Norton, New York.

Follet, M.P. [1920], The new state: Group organization, the solution of popular government, lonmans green, London.

Fombrun, C.Tichy, N.M and Devanna, M.A. [1984], strategic human resources management, Wiley, New York.

Ford, H. [1922], My life and work, Heinemann, London.

French, J. and Raven, B. (1959), "the bases of social power", in D. Cartwright (ed.), Studies in Social Power, Institute for Social Research, Ann Arbor, MI.

Friedman, M. (1962), Capitalism and Freedom, University of Chicago Press, Chicago.

Gabrial, Y. (1988), Working Lives in Catering, Routledge, London.

Gerwin, D. (1979), "Relationships between structures and technology at the organizational and job levels", Journal of Management Studies, vol. 16, no.1, pp. 70-79.

Ghoshal, S. And Bartlett, C.A. (1998), The Individualized Corporation, Heinemann, London.

Gilbreth, L.M. (1914), The Psychology of Management, Sturgis & Walton, New York.

Gillespie, R. (1991), Manufacturing Knowledge: A history of the Hawthorne experiments, Cambridge University press, Cambridge.

Gitman L. (1985) Managerial finance 4th edition.

Glaister, K.W. (1991), 'Virgin Atlantic Airways', in C. Clark-Hill and K. Glaister, Cases in Strategic Management, Pitman, London.

Glaister, K.W. and Falshaw, J.R. (1999), 'Strategic Planning: still going strong?' Long Range Planning, vol. 32, no. 1, pp. 107-116.

Glass, N. (1996), 'Chaos, non-linear systems and day-to-day management', European Management Journal, vol. 14, no. 1, pp. 98-106.

Goldratt, E. and Cox, J. (1989), The Goal, Gower, Aldershot.

Goold, M. (1997), 'Institutional advantage: a way into strategic management in not-for-profit organizations', Long Range Planning, vol. 30, no. 2, pp. 291-293.

Govindarajan, V. And Gupta, A.k. (2001), 'Building an effective global business team'. MIT Sloan Management Review, vol. 42, no. 4, pp. 63-72.

Graham, P. (1995), Mary Parker Follett: Prophet of management, Harvard Bussiness School Press, Boston, MA.

Grant S T (2004) Introuction to Economics (6th Edition) Longman.

Grant, S. T. (2004) Introuction to Economics (6th Edition) Longman.

Grant, R. (2002), Contemporary Strategy Analysis (4th edn), Blackwell, Oxford.

Grant, R.M. (1991), 'The resource-based theory of competitive advantage: implications for strategy formulation', California Management Review, vol. 33, no. 3, pp. 114-135.

Greem, Mark. (1983), Risk management, Text and Cases N Y.

Greenberg, J. (1990), 'Employee theft as a reaction to underpayment inequity: the hidden costs of pay cuts', Journal of Applied Psychology, vol. 75, no. 5, pp. 561-568.

Greenwood, R.G., Bolton, A.A. and Greenwood, R.A. (1983), 'Hawthorne a half century Later: relay assembly participants remember', Journal of Management, vol. 9, Fall/Winter, pp. 217-231.

Greer, C.R. (2001), Strategic Human Resource Management, Prentice Hall, New Jersey.

Gronroos, C. (2000), Service Management and Marketing: A customer relationship management approach (2nd edn), Wiley, Chichester.

Guest, D. (1988), 'Human resource management: a new opportunity for psychologist or another passing fad?' The Occupational Psychologist, February.

Guest, D.E. (1987), 'Human resource management and industrial relations', Journal of Management Studies, vol. 24, no. 5, pp. 502-521.

Guest, D.E. and Conway, N. (2001), Organisational change and the Psychological Contract: An analysis of the 1999 CIPD Survey, Chartered Institute of Personnel and Development, London.

Guirdham, M. (1995), Interpersonal Skills at work, Prentice Hall International, Hemel Hempstead.

Gyory Robert. The future of risk management, in risk managemet V11

Habermas, J. (1972), Knowledge and Human Interests, Heinemann, London.

Hackham et al. (1975), 'Development of the job diagnostic survey', Journal of Applied Psychology, vol. 60, no.2, p. 161.

Hackham, J.R. (1990), Groups that Work (and those that don't), Jossey-Bass, San Francisco, CA.

Hackham, J.R. and Oldham, G.R. (1980), Work Redesign, Addison-Wesley, Reading, MA.

Hage, J. and Aiken, M. (1967), 'Program change and organizational properties: a comparative analysis', American Journal of Sociology, vol. 72, pp.503-519.

Hagman, E. (2000), Keynote address to Arthur Anderson European Business and Environment Network Annual Conference, 15 September.

Hales, C. (2001), Managing through Organization, Routledge, London.

Hall, W. (1995), Managing Cultures, Wiley, Chichester.

Hamel, G. And Prahald, C.K. (1996), Competing for the Future, Harvard Business School Press, Boston, MA.

Handbook of Management (2004,) (3rd Edition), FT Prentice

Handy, C. (1988), Understanding Voluntary Organizations, Penguin, Harmondsworth.

Handy, C. (1993), Understanding Organizations (4th edn), Penguin, Harmondsworth.

Hannagan, T. (2008), Management Concepts and Practices (5th) Edition FT Prentice Hal.l.

Hanson Edward.(1986) Rreducing Insurance cost through risk management

Hardaker, M. and Ward, B. (1987), 'getting things done', Harvard Business Review, vol. 65, no. 6, pp. 112-120.

Hargie, O. et al (2004), Communication Skills for Effective Management, Palgrave.

Hargie, O.D.W. (1997), Handbook of Communication Skills, Routledge, London.

Harris, P.R. and Moran, R. (1991), Managing Cultural Differences, Gulf Publishing, Houston, TX.

Harrison, E. F. (1999), The Managerial Decision. Making Process (5th edn), Houghton Mifflin, Boston, MA.

Hartley, J. Bennington, J. and Binns, P. (1997), 'Researching the roles of internal change agents in the management of organizational change', British Journal of Management, vol. 8, no. 1, pp. 61-74.

Hawcult, P. (1982), Captive insurance company. Establishment, Operation, and Managementm, NY.

Heil, G., Bennis, W. and Stephens, D.C. (2000), Douglas McGregor, Revisited, Wiley, New York.

Helgesen, S. (1995), The Female Advantage: Women's way of leadership, Currency/Doubleday, New York.

Heller, R. (2001),'inside Zara', Forbes Global, 28 May, pp. 24-25, 28-29.

Hellriegel, D. and Slocum, J (1988), Management (5th edn), Addison-Wesley, Readig, MA.

Hellriegel, D., Jackson, S.E. and Slocum, J.w. (2002), Management: A competency-based approach, South Western College Publishing, Cincinatti, OH.

Henderson, D. (2001), Misguided Virtue: False notions of coporate social responsibility, Institute of Economic Affairs, London.

Herzberg, F. (1959), The Motivation to Work, Wiley, New York.

Herzberg, F. (1987), 'One more time: how do you motivate employees?' Harvard Business Review, vol. 65, no. 5, pp. 109-120.

Heydebrand, W.V. (1989), 'New organisational forms', Work and Occupations, vol. 16, no. 3, pp. 323-357.

Hill, C.W.L. and Pickering, J.F. (1986), 'Divisionlization, decentralization and performance of large United Kingdom companies', Journal of Management Studies, vol. 23, no. 1, pp. 26-50.

Hill, T. (2004), Operations Management (2nd edn), Palgrave Macmillan, London.

Hiltrop, J.M. (1995), 'The Changing psychological contract: the human resources challenge of the 1990s', European Management Journal, vol.13, no. 3, pp. 288-294.

Hofstede, G. (1980) Culture's Consequences: International differences in work-related values, Sage, Beverley Hills, CA.

Hofstede, G. (1989), 'Organizing for cultural diversity', European Management Journal, vol. 7, no. 4, pp. 390-397.

Hofstede, G. (1991), Cultures and Organisations: Softweare of the mind, McGraw-Hill, London.

Honderich, T. (ed.) (1995), Ethical Reasoning:The Oxford Companion to Philosophy, Oxford University Press, Oxford.

Hoppe, M.H. (1993), 'The effects of national culture on the theory and practice of managing R&D professionals abroad', R&D Management, vol. 23, no. 4,pp. 313-325.

Horngren, C.T., Foster, G. And Datar, S.M. (2002), Cost Accounting (10th edn), Financial Times/Prentice Hall, Harlow.

House, R.J. (1996), 'Path-goal theory of leadership: lessons, legacy and a reformulation', Leadership Quarterly, vol. 7, no.3, pp. 323-352.

House, R.J. and Mitchell, T.R. (1974), 'Path-goal theory of leadership', Contemporary Business, vol. 3, no. 2, pp. 81-98.

Howard, J.A. and Sheth, J.N. (1969), The Theory of Buyer Behaviour, Wiley, New York.

Howard, P. (1999), 'Fair play is better businesses, Business Review Weekly, March.

Huczynski, A.A.(2004), Influencing Within Organizations (2nd edn), Routledge, London.

Hueber S, (1982) Insurance development, in annuals of the American academy of polical and social science, philadephia.

Huselid, M.A. (1995), 'The impact of human resource management practices on turnover, productivity and corporate financial performance', Academy of Management Journal, vol. 38, no. 3, pp. 635-672.

Ibbott, C. and O'keefe, R. (2004), 'Transforming the Vodafone/ Ericsson relationship', Long Range Planning, vol. 37, no. 3, pp. 219-237.

Ichniowski, C., Kochan, T.A., Levine, D., Olson, C. and Strauss, G. (1996), 'What works at work: overview and assessment', Industrial Relations, vol. 35, no. 3, pp. 299-333.

IPD (1999), Organisational development: whose responsibility? Institute for Personnel and Development, London.

IRS (1997), 'The state of selection: an IRS survey', Employee Development Bulletin, 51, pp. 5-8, Industrial Relations Services, London.

Isobe, l Dole & Robin Lowe (2004), International Marketing Strategy (4th Edition) Thomson.

Jackson, T. (1993), Organizational Behaviour in International Management, Butterworth/ Heinemann, Oxford.

Janis, I. L. (1977), Decision Making: A psychological analysis of conflict, choice and commitment, The Free Press, New York.

Janis, I. (1972), Victim of Groupthink, Houghton-Mufflin, Boston, MA.

Jennings, D. (2000),'PowerGen: the development of corporate planning in a privatized utility', Long Range Planning, vol. 33, no. 2, pp. 201-219.

Jobber, D. (2004), Principles and Practices of Marketing (4th edn), McGraw-Hill, London.

John, K.A., Northcraft, G.B. and Neale, M.A. (1999), 'Why differences make a differenc: a field study of diversity, conflict and performance in work groups', Adminstrative Scinece Quartely, vol. 44, no. 4, pp. 741-763

Johnson, G, (1986) Strategic Change and the Management Trocess, New Yprk,

Johnson, G. and Scholes, K. (2001), Exploring Corporate Strategy (6th edn), Financial Times/Prentice Hall, Harlow.

Johnson, G. and Scholes, K. (eds.) (2002), Exploring Public Sector Strategy, Prentice Hall, Harlow.

Johnston, R.A., Kast, F.E. and Rosenweig, J.E. (19667), 'people and systems', in -The Theory and Management of Systems, McGraw-Hill, New York.

Jones, J. R., George J. M. (2010). Contemporary Management (3rd Edition), McGraw Hill.

Judd, V.C. (2003), 'Achieving customer orientation using people power- the 5th P', European Journal of Marketing, vol. 37, no. 10, pp. 1301-1313.

Judge, T.A. Piccolo, R.F. and Ilies, R. (2004), 'The forgotten ones? The validity of consideration and initiating structure in leadership resaerch', Journal of Applied Psychology, vol. 89, no. 1, pp.36-51

Juran, J. [1974], quality control Handbook, McGrew-Hill, New York

Kakabadse, A. [1993], 'the succecsss levers for Europe: the Cranfield executive competence survey', journal of management development, vol. 12, no. 8, pp.12 – 17.

Kanter, R.M. [1979] 'Power failure in management circuits' Harvard business review, vol. 57, no. 4, pp. 65 – 75.

Kanter, R.M. [1983], the change masters, Unwin, London.

Kaplan, R.S. and Norton, D.P 1996], the balanced scorecard: translating strategy into action, Harvard business school press, Cambridge, MA.

Kaplan, S. [2000], 'E-Hubs: the new B2B marketplace', Harvard business review, vol. 78, no.3, pp. 97 – 113.

Katzenbach, J. R. and Smith, D.K 1993a], "the discipline of teams", Harvard business review, vol. 71, no.2, pp. 111– 120.

Katzenbach, J. R. and Smith, D.K 1993b]," wisdom of teams", Harvard business school press, Boston.

Kay, J. [1993], foundations for corporate success: how business strategies add value, oxford university press, oxford.

Kay, J. [1996], "the business of economics", Oxford University Press, Oxford.

Keaveney, P. and Kaufmann, M.[2001], marketing for the voluntary sector, kogan page, London.

Keef, S.P. [1998], 'the casual association between employee share ownership and attitudes', British jounal of industrial relations, vol. 36, no.1, pp. 73 – 82.

Keegaan, warren (2004) Global Marketing (4th Edition) Prentice hall.

Keen, P. [1981], 'information systems and organisation change', in E. Rhodes and D. wields [eds], implementing new technologies, Blackwell/open university press, oxford.

Klien, G. [1997], cources of power: how people make decisions, MIT press, Cambridge, MA.

Klien, N. [2000], "No logo": Taking aim at the brand bullies, Flamingo, London.

Kliener, A. [2003],who really matters: the core group theory of power privilege and success, Doubleday, New York.

Kloman, H. (1984)Captive insurance company; in risk management report

Knapp, M. L. and Hall, J [2002], Non-Verbal Communication in Human Interactions, Thomson learnig, London.

Knights, D. and Murray, F. [1994], managers divided: organisational politics and information technology management, Wiley, Chichester.

Kochan, T.A. [1992], "Principle for a post new-deal employment policy", Sloan School of Management, MIT, working paper 5.

Kochan, T.A. et al. [2003] 'the effect of diversity on business performance: report of the diversity research network', Human resource management, vol. 42, no.1, pp. 3 – 21.

Kolb, D. Rubin, E. and Osland, J. [1991], organisational psychology, Prentice Hall, Englewood Cliffs, NJ.

Komaki, J. [2003], 'Reinforcement theory at work: enhaceind and explaining what workers do', in L.W. porter, G.A. B igley and R.M steers [eds], motivation and work behaviour [7th edn], Irwin/McGrew-Hill, Burr Ridge, IL.

Komaki, J.L. Coombs, T. Redding, T.P. and Schepman, S. [2000],'A rich and rigorous examination of applied behaviour analysis research in the world of work', in C.L. Cooper and I.T. Robertson [eds], international review of industrial and organisational psychology, Wiley, Chichester, pp. 265 – 367.

Kotler, P. [2003], Marketing Management [11th edn], Pearson Education, Upper Saddle river, NJ.

Kotler, P. Armstrong, G. [1997], Marketing: An introduction [4th edn], Prentice Hall International, Hemel Hampstead.

Kotler, P. Armstrong, G. Saunders, J. and Wong, V. [2002], Principles of Marketing [3rd European edn], Financial Times/Prentice Hall, Harlow.

Kottasz, R. [2004], 'how should charitable organisations motivate young professionals to give philanthropically?', international journal of non- profit and voluntary sector marketing, vol. 9, no.1, pp. 9 – 27.

Kotter, J.P. [1982], The General Manager, free press, New York.

Kotter, J.P. [1991], A force for change: how leadership differs from management, the free press, New York.

Kotter, J.P. and Heskett, J. [1992], corporate culture and performance, free press, New York.

Kotter, J.P. and Schlesinger, L.A. [1979], 'choosing strategies for change', Harvard business review, vol. 57, no.3, pp. 106 – 114.

Kotter, J. and Cohen, D. [2002], the heart of change: real life stories of how people change their organisations, Harvard business school press, Boston, MA.

Krackhardt, D. and Hanson, J.R. [1993],' informal networks: the companies behind the charts', Harvard business review, vol. 71, no.4, pp. 104 – 111.

Lancaster, G. and Messingham, L. [1993], Essentials of Marketing [2nd edn], McGrew-Hill, New York.

Laudon, K.C and Laudon, J.P. [2004], management information systems: managing the digital firm [8nd edn], Principle Hall, Upper Saddle River, NJ.

Laurie, J. Mullins (2010), Management and Organisational Behaviour (9th edition) FT Prentice Hall.

Linstead, S. et al (2004), Management and Organisations- Palgrave.

Mintzberg (1973), The Nature of Management Work, Harper&Row.

Naylor J (2004) management – An Introduction (2nd Edition) Pearson

Needle, D. (2002), Business in Context (3th Edition), Thompson.

NHS constitution (2011) NHS Publication.

Philip, Kotler (2006), Marketing Manage net (6thEdition) Prentice Hall

Philip, Kotler (2004) Principles of Management (5th Edition) Prentice hall

Rosebaum, D. (1981), Captive Insurance Company Report VIII, Pproperly and Liability Insurance- Captive insurance Company Review 1981.

Stokes, D. (2006), Small Business Management (4thEdition) Continuum.

Sutherland, J. et al (2004), Key Concepts in Management, Palgrave.

Vaughan E (1986), Fundamentals of risk management and insurance (4th Edition) New York.

www.ingramcontent.com/pod-product-compliance
Lightning Source LLC
Chambersburg PA
CBHW030917180526
45163CB00002B/364